# Laughing at Life's Most Embarrassing Moments

## DAN TAYLOR

**HARVEST HOUSE PUBLISHERS**
EUGENE, OREGON

Cover by Dugan Design Group

Back cover author photo by Ellen T Stewart

**Laughing at Life's Most Embarrassing Moments**
Copyright © 2018 by Dan Taylor
Published by Harvest House Publishers
Eugene, Oregon 97408
www.harvesthousepublishers.com

ISBN 978-0-7369-2464-1 (pbk.)
ISBN 978-0-7369-5020-6 (eBook)

Library of Congress Cataloging-in-Publication Data

Names: Taylor, Dan, author.
Title: Laughing at life's most embarrassing moments / Dan Taylor.
Description: Eugene, Oregon : Harvest House Publishers, 2018.
Identifiers: LCCN 2018008259 (print) | LCCN 2018009526 (ebook) | ISBN
  9780736950206 (ebook) | ISBN 9780736924641 (paperback)
Subjects: LCSH: Christian life—Humor. | Conduct of life—Humor. | BISAC:
  RELIGION / Christian Life / General. | HUMOR / General.
Classification: LCC BV4517 (ebook) | LCC BV4517 .T38 2018 (print) | DDC
  242—dc23
LC record available at https://lccn.loc.gov/2018008259

**Printed in the United States of America**

18  19  20  21  22  23  24  25  26  / BP-GL /  10  9  8  7  6  5  4  3  2  1

# Contents

# Trying to Find the Funny

Cool guys are everywhere. They're on billboards as you drive down the road. They're on your television on literally hundreds of channels. And today, all the cool guys who ever existed digitally can keep on existing forever. They're even on your phone—*the phone in your pocket!* We are surrounded on all sides by seemingly endless waves of coolness.

It's been like this my entire life, so it's no surprise that, growing up, I wanted some of that coolness. And that coolness wasn't just out there in the "worldly world" either. As a preacher's kid, I quickly learned that Sunday school teachers can be cool. And youth ministers. And speakers at rallies where cool worship bands played beforehand. Those speakers embodied coolness as they told us that all the heroes in the Bible were very, very cool.

But here's the thing about being cool: The harder you try to attain it, the more elusive it becomes. And when you miss…well, it's worse than not trying at all. There's a kind of failure that comes from trying something you didn't believe you could do anyway. You end up making things doubly, or triply, or…whatever is four times, *worse.*

What do you do when you've failed to navigate the oval at the skating rink? What do you do when algebra has once again beaten you in a battle of wits, this time on a blackboard in front of an entire class? What do you do when you find yourself trapped in a vending machine or driving a bus whose wheels are no longer touching the ground? You laugh. You laugh as if it was all part of a big, mysterious plan.

Then you try to get other people to laugh. When we're laughing, nothing scary seems as scary. Nothing bad seems as bad. When we're laughing together, at least we're *together.* And who knows? Maybe something better is about to happen.

This is the story of me, trying to find the funny parts of pretty much everything. Because I've learned that if we can laugh at the hardest and most embarrassing parts of life, then laughing at the rest of it is easy.

# 1

# Carsick? Must Be Sunday

When I was a child, I thought going to church made *everyone* carsick. You know, the unpleasantly nautical feeling that the family car (never a van—they weren't invented for families yet, and we were not hippies) is kind of floating, and you might or might not be giving back the parent-approved, non-sugary cereal you had for breakfast?

Every Sunday, that was me, riding in the back of the car with my brother and sister. Ostensibly in charge as the oldest and taking that responsibility very seriously, this was awkward for me. It's hard enough to lead with no real authority and with the people who are actually in charge just one seat ahead of you, but when you just want to lie very still with a cool cloth on your forehead until the boat docks...well, it's not an effective power play.

Why would God do this? Make his servants sickly each Sunday? It was a mystery to me. I would bob along in the *SS Sedan*, wondering how the waves of nausea fit into the plan for our lives and why everyone else wasn't complaining.

This happened every Sunday we went to church, which was 52 Sundays a year. Looking back, it never occurred to me that going to church had something to do with my dad's job. It was just what we did. In fact, it's what most of the people I knew did. I knew that the guy speaking up front was my dad, and I knew the church had a pastor. Yet somehow I failed to put those two things together.

The preacher guy in front of the congregation wasn't the same guy who would later toss me in the air and tuck me into my bunk bed. I mean, he was, but only sort of. Away from church, he was a regular guy. I didn't think of him as "clergy," even though we had a sticker on the car that got us enviable hospital parking. David Taylor was certainly not better than anyone else in any way. I understood that God loved us all the same, even though at church, my dad preached and my mom, Delores, played the piano. That's just how it was.

Kids don't know that exceptional things are exceptions, so I thought everybody went to church. Everybody in our congregation did their part there—ushering, deaconing, eldering, bringing potluck dishes to potluck dinners, setting up chairs, taking down chairs, and boxing up hymnals. My family just happened to be the ones who left last and locked the doors on the way out.

All this brings us back to why I was carsick. My family always ate breakfast before we headed to church. Then it was about a half hour in the backseat of the car, and…bingo! (Only, not really bingo, because we weren't Catholics. I mean bingo, carsickness, which is not nearly as much fun as real bingo.)

I don't remember much about my BC (before church) days. As far as I know, I was always either in church, on the way there, or on the way home from there. For the pastor's family, church is Sunday morning, Sunday night, Wednesday night, and all the other various times our presence was required.

There were early signs this would be the case. One of them started about as early as possible—right about the time I was named "Daniel."

# 2

# Methuselah Jr.

When your parents give you a Bible name, they give you a burden (even though they probably don't mean to). It's not a "bad news about your barns and lands and relatives, Job" kind of burden, but a nagging, everyday burden, which you could argue is exactly what parents are for!

As far as Bible names go, Daniel isn't bad. Could be a lot, lot, worse. Melchizedek is *way* out there. At least Daniel came with some options. When I was a kid, nobody used the longer or more formal versions of their names. Every Charles was Charlie. Every William was Billy. No Daniel was Daniel. For the first 19 or 20 years, I was Danny. That ended when I entered adulthood without becoming a used-car salesman.

If you are an adult Danny, you have to be a super fun guy. You should know a bunch of card games involving spoons. You must know lots of age- and audience-appropriate jokes and at least a couple of magic tricks. It's a lot of pressure. We "Dans" don't have that weighing us down.

In Hebrew, Daniel means "God is my judge." This name imbued me with a kind of gravitas that the other bundles of joy in the delivery room didn't share. They were getting measured and weighed and drinking however many ounces of formula. Meanwhile, I was being, you know, judged by God.

How popular was Daniel, aka Danny, in my birth year? Well, 19 years later I was on a soccer team at a small Bible school. (The school was small; the Bibles were regular sized.) And let me just quickly say that we were terrible and were ceremonially slaughtered on unsanctified fields across the Midwest. I bring it up because there were four—*four!*—Dans on the team. If someone yelled, "Your ball, Dan!" he was probably right. In the inevitable postgame debrief, blaming the loss on a Dan was pretty much a sure thing.

The other popular Bible name going at the time was, of course, Michael. That's the prize, as far as Bible names. In Hebrew, Michael means "Who is like God?" so it's kind of a rhetorical gauntlet you throw down whenever you sign something. Further, Michael was an archangel, while Daniel was just a prophet. Daniel had lions, sure. That's cool. But the archangel Michael? He was a leader and a fierce warrior with a sword and everything. Daniel merely avoided getting eaten by lions.

Also popular at the time was Timothy, which is a fine name. However, Timothy was Paul's sidekick, right? So, why not just name your kid Paul if you're heading that way?

And can anyone explain Thomas? The dude is famous for doubting. *Doubting*. Yet, how many Toms and Tommys did I know? A lot. Same for David and John. When I was a kid, you couldn't swing a dead cat (never named David or John) without hitting someone with one or the other of these monikers.

Today, ironically, you rarely find a newborn Daniel or a Michael or a Timothy or even a Thomas. These days, it's all about Josiah.

Josiah? In Hebrew, Josiah means "Jehovah has healed." Josiah was a king of Judah at age eight, so props for that. When I was eight, I was still mastering riding around the neighborhood on two wheels.

I know several newborn Micahs, and I'll encounter an occasional Jonah and even a Noah, which both seem oddly nautical for babies born in Kansas, where I live. But that's not the kind of thing you point out to a mom in a delivery room.

These are all biblical boy names, of course. Nowadays you can be trendy and give a girl what used to be a boy's name. Micah, for example, can go from blue to pink in a blink.

For girls, choosing a Bible name is much easier. You have Elizabeth, and her cousin Mary, for the most part. Deborah and Sarah had a phenomenal reign. Ruth also had a good run. But Liz and Mary dominate.

And, of course, if you really want to get creative, there's always Dani.

# 3

# Community Juice

When I was eight, something important happened at church. It was important then, but it became even more important later.

I got baptized.

In our church's tradition, baptism means full immersion. You step into a tank or a tub or a lake or a pool and go 100 percent underwater. But when to take the plunge? That's the big question.

It's easy for guys in jail. At least that's what I thought as a kid. Gang members, drug addicts, and bank robbers—they could say, "I'm going to quit this gang and these drugs and this robbing. I'm gonna repent and get baptized!"

But when you're a pastor's kid, as I was, it's a little trickier. You know you want to turn from a life of sin, but to be honest, you haven't had a lot of opportunities for sin. You've learned about the Bible heroes who repented and got baptized, and there's this polite assumption: "Of course little Danny wants to repent and get baptized!" But at age eight, you're hard-pressed to name exactly what you need to repent *from*. Your opportunities for bank robbing or a thug life in general are rare.

I'd first considered getting "bap-a-tized" before I could even pronounce the word correctly. I wanted to be baptized for a very simple reason: community juice (aka Communion grape juice). The grown-ups got to drink that delicious purple beverage every Sunday. I wanted in on that action.

When I first expressed my desire to my parents, they explained that, while my six-year-old heart was probably in right place, there was more to Communion than the juice. They told me I'd understand, as was the case with so many things, "when I was older."

So, two years later, I was good to go. I was a very mature eight. I understood many Bible stories and their applications to my life. Also, my girlfriend, Kim Johansen, was getting baptized, so I wanted to as well.

How does an eight-year-old have a girlfriend? Only in that adorable, little-kid way. I wouldn't have a real girlfriend for another four years. (Spoiler alert: My relationship with Tanya Krzynowski would not last long.)

Anyway, my eight-year-old girl, Kim, was getting baptized, and I now knew how to pronounce the word correctly. It was time.

In our church, baptism worked like this: My dad finished the sermon with what we called an "invitation." Other churches call it an altar call, but we were nondenominational enough to not have an altar, just a table.

Anyway, the sermon wrapped up and there was an invitation hymn. It was just one of the regular hymns but sung at the end of the service. Kim and I walked nervously toward the front of the sanctuary. Dad came down a step or two and greeted us. Then he asked us if we wanted to get baptized. We said yes. He sent us off, directing Kim to one side of the not-altar area and me to the other.

Kim and I finally found ourselves in that mysterious "behind the pulpit" area! What wonders would await? Basically, it was just a closet on either side of what amounted to a very small indoor pool or a very large bathtub.

Soon we were wearing the swimsuits our moms had placed in the closets, and we put robes on over them. Dad was already in the water. He was wearing waders over his suit pants. This was so that he could, superhero-style, exit the water and get to the back of the church in time to shake everyone's hand once the baptism was over. My family knew I was "coming forward" that morning. Kim's family knew she was. But the congregation had no heads-up, so we had to keep things moving. There were pot roasts in ovens.

Both of us stood together in the water with my dad. Kim went first. I was so nervous that I hardly noticed anything but our robes, moving in the water like jellyfish.

Then it was my turn. Pastor/Dad asked very seriously, but also with a very big proud smile on his face, if I wanted to be baptized. I say I did. Next thing I know, I was underwater for a couple of seconds and then back up, sputtering, getting hugged, and trying to navigate the steps while being tugged toward the bottom by a very wet robe.

Six hours later, the very coolest part happened.

Our church did Communion every Sunday morning, but you had to be baptized to be eligible to drink the "community juice." As Kim and I were not baptized until *after* Communion, there was no juice for us that morning.

However, we did get to *take Communion that night!*

The only people who got to do this were the rebels, the renegades, the people who, for whatever reason, were not able to make it to church in the morning. So we came to the night service. The night service had the singing, but not the offering. There was a short sermon and a quick serving of Communion *at night*.

You would walk to the front pew, sit down, and, after a quick prayer, here came the trays.

It's hard to convey to the adult mind what this meant to a kid like me. *Who were these other people who had not been at church that morning?* I wondered. *Where had they been? What kind of jobs prevented someone from being in church from 9:30 to noon? Secret agents? Brain surgeons? Secret brain surgeons?*

I sat among them, trying to look cool, trying to convey that their secrets were safe with me. The tray of tiny crackers was passed to me. I took one and ate it. Then came the tray of tiny juice cups. I took one and drank it.

That night, I received more than the Communion elements. I was part of something. Something big and powerful and special. Something that made my dad smile when he prayed the benediction that morning from the water. Something that made my mom pray for me in a deeper, different way. Something that did, does, and, in a way, always will, define me.

# 4

# Church Clothes Woes

Not only did I get to see the cool, mysterious nighttime Communion takers on Sunday nights, but I also got to wear my own clothes.

The clothes I had to wear on Sunday mornings were also mine, technically. But they never *felt* like mine. They had their own place in the closet, where they stayed Monday through Saturday. Even though *hate* was a word we were not supposed to say, I *hated* those clothes.

I hated the pants. I hated the shirts. But I really, especially, hated the shoes. Church shoes were not, and could never be, anything close to athletic shoes. No Red Ball Jets, no Chuck Taylor Converse, and no Keds. If it was allowed on a basketball court, it was not allowed at church. Church shoes were basically a pair of matching torture devices. If kids knew the launch codes, you could threaten them with church shoes, and they would quickly give up those codes. (That's just one of many good reasons not to give kids launch codes.)

I hated my church shoes. That might have had something to do with the fact that I was always losing my church shoes.

Sunday mornings at our house were tense, militaristic endeavors. A lot of moving parts had to work in seamless synchronization to get three kids out the door early enough to set up whatever needed setting up that Sunday. Breakfast made and eaten, beds made, hair plastered into place and, of course, outfits organized and donned.

The shirt and pants spent all week hanging in the closet untouched— no problem finding them. But the shoes? Where did the shoes go? To this day, I can't say. But they migrated; that's for sure. Were they under the bed? Good news! One was. Where was the other? How could I possibly know? At the bottom of the toy box? Behind the hamper? In the basement? The shoe could be anywhere. Threats, tears, bargaining—basically all the stages of grief were experienced every Sunday morning as we gathered as a family to tear apart the house to find the missing shoe. Now, if only I could find my belt…

. . . . . . . . . . . . .

My brother, sister, and I usually constituted the entire youth group. But sometimes our church would include another couple of families with kids around our ages. This was both a blessing and a curse. Other kids? Yay! That's mostly how we looked at it. But sometimes a kid would be odd or mean or both, and we still had to be friends with him or her. It's like having a cellmate, I suppose. You must attempt to be friends or it's super awkward all day.

One year, our church had maybe a half dozen kids who were politely pretending to be friends, and it was almost Christmas. Guess what's coming? If you are good at guessing, you have correctly guessed: a Christmas pageant.

I believe I was a shepherd at my first pageant. Or possibly Joseph. It's all a blur, this brush with the craft of live theater. I remember a towel tied around my head and an adult bathrobe brushing the tile floor of the community center our church rented each Sunday. A girl in an identical towel and robe getup, playing Mary, was holding a *real* baby, whom someone had recently birthed and immediately put into religious showbiz.

An angel (white robe, cardboard wings) and maybe another shepherd or two milled around the building until an adult with Spielbergian leanings herded us into the kitchen area and then sent us onstage, as the reading of Matthew dictated. It was very moving and adorable, judging by the moved and adoring looks on the faces of the crowd. Tragically, no one in the church had a videocamera, much less a phone that could record everything. But take my word for it: Lives were changed that day. At least mine was. It became crystal clear to me that morning that I had no gift whatsoever for live theater.

Once the pageant was over, we boxed up the Bibles and folded the folding chairs. We had enjoyed a taste of the bright lights. (Metaphorically speaking, of course. The lights at the community center had only two settings: off and on.) However, we learned that fame was fleeting.

Take off the towel and the bathrobe and, whether you portrayed a shepherd or Joseph, you were really just a kid in the church clothes you hated.

Especially the shoes.

# 5

# Youth Group of Three

Megachurches, their imposing appearances to the contrary, have not been with us forever. Satellite churches are, likewise, relatively new. What you used to have to do if you wanted a church where there wasn't one was simple: Plant a church.

Yes, just like a tree or a shrub or the subtle idea that your husband's mustache just isn't working, a church has to be planted. This requires the services of a church planter. For a big part of my growing-up years, that's what my dad did.

And like a tree or a shrub or a successful getting-rid-of-that-ridiculous-mustache plot, planted churches start very small.

Oddly, these churches are not small on their official first Sunday. On that day, the larger churches send emissaries to the "new plant," so it looks like things are off to a big start. "Hooray!" the people exclaim. (Or, if they're really spiritual, "Hallelujah!")

Not until the second Sunday do you realize what you're actually dealing with.

My dad's church plants usually comprised only a few families. Some came from other churches, agreeing to stick with the new effort for a few months to "fill out the roster." A few other people lived close to the new church and were excited not to have to drive so far and risk burning their pot roasts before they made it home.

As for the youth group? Well, as I mentioned earlier, the youth "group" was typically composed of just three kids—me; my brother, Damon; and my sister, DeeAnn. Our whole group fit into a Datsun B210. If you've never seen such a vehicle, it's even smaller than you imagine.

Some churches, I would find out later, had a youth group bus. A bus! You could put three Datsun B210s on a bus and still have room for a mobile board meeting.

For a youth group of three kids, epic water balloon battles are out of the question. The same goes for capture the flag and flag football.

Our youth group activities were limited to setting up folding chairs before church and then unpacking Bibles and hymnals and putting them on the recently unfolded chairs. Then we were encouraged to sit still. Occasionally, we were allowed to draw quietly or see how many new words we could make from "Announcements" and other words we could find in the bulletin. Then it was time to pack up again.

With virtually no other youth group members, we Taylor kids were on our own. It was kind of like being a missionary kid right in the middle of the USA. (Incidentally, I know many missionary kids. Like a preacher's kids, they go one of two directions. Either they grow up to become the most well-rounded, interesting, smart, and confident people on the planet, or they become shy and awkward adults. By "shy and awkward," I mean weird.)

I was an Option B person myself. That proved to be unfortunate, because, as the senior member of the youth group and the oldest child of our fishbowl family, I had to meet a lot of people. Really a lot. Hundreds.

I got good at it. I could shake hands "like I meant it," just as my dad taught me. I could look grown-ups in the eye and answer their questions in full sentences, but it filled me with dread. To set the scene, here's me for most of my childhood, featured in the following play...

### THIS HAPPENS EVERY SUNDAY (A One-Act Play)

Setting: The curtain opens on a small congregation where a service has just ended. DAN, a shy, scrawny youngster, is corralling the youth group (his younger brother and sister) as MOM washes tiny Communion cups. DAD approaches. He is smiling and talking to STRANGER, another adult.

**DAN** (to self)
Please don't make me meet this person, please don't make me meet this person, please don't make me meet this person...

**DAD**
And this is my number one son, Danny!

**DAN**
(*Firmly shaking STRANGER's hand*) Nice to meet you.

**STRANGER**
You are tall, and your father is short.

**DAN**
Ha-ha, yes! I have to go now.

And... *scene.*

Repeat one thousand million times. That's not an exaggeration. I have a calculator on my phone, and I figured it out.

People loved the idea that I was tall for my age, while Dad was not very tall. People found this fascinating. They just couldn't get over it. They always had to comment. Eventually, my brother, Damon, would also prove to be slightly taller than average, and Dad would introduce us as his bodyguards. People loved that too.

Years later, I figured out that when adults walk up to a kid, they have no idea what to say. I learned this by being an adult who walked up to kids with no idea what to say. I've written a short play about that too...

**DAN TAYLOR WALKING UP TO A KID** (A One-Act Play)

**DAN**
Hi! Um, electronic dance rave music? Pokémon Kombat 3? How's school? Good? Sports?

**EVERY KID, EVER**
Ha-ha, yes! I have to go now.

And... *scene.*

# 6

# Covered Dishes, Childhood Wishes

The preacher's kids must greet people at church. I get that now, but as a kid, I just thought adults were all kind of the same good-natured people who were happy to meet me and wanted to know what sports I played (none at the time) and how school was going (terrifying) and how I got so tall. The social anxiety of my weekly ritual of having to greet people at church was broken up every now and then by the glory that was…potluck dinners!

Like most kids, I wasn't an adventurous eater. I ate bologna and hot dogs and…well, that's about it. Ground-up animals, mostly, interspersed with the occasional PB&J. So potluck dinners at church would have been a great opportunity for me to try any number of things. I'm sure that many delicious things were there to try, but I have no memory of them. That's because entire tables of food were eclipsed by the sheer culinary magnetism of store-bought cookies! And they were the good ones, the primo stuff. I mean the kind that start with an O and end with O and have REally good stuff in the middle.

Desserts, in a moving visual depiction of "the first will be last," were at the far end of the two banquet tables that were set up in the fellowship hall, or what passed for one in the rental buildings. There were cobblers and cakes and pies, but none of that mattered because some pressed-for-time mom (never a dad; it was the 1970s and we weren't hippies) would flout tradition and "just" bring a bag of store-bought bounty.

Those quote marks around "just" are to indicate the narrow thinking of the other moms. From their lofty adult perches, they looked down on the store and the buying of cookies. Why? There's nothing like hearth and home, that's for sure, but unless your last name is Oreo and you've just come up with something that's about to change lives, your kitchen

20

has limits. Mash your potatoes. Blanch your beans. Put whatever you can think of into that Jell-O mold. But then go to the store and buy the round, black cookies with the white insides, the ones that you've seen on TV. Do this, and you will be buying the gratitude of all the kids at the upcoming potluck dinner. They are counting on you.

My siblings and I were under strict orders to fill our plate with a vegetable and some kind of protein, which at the time was untrendily called "meat." Then, and only then, could we claim a dessert.

This was a bit tricky.

Meaning no offense to all the moms who were not my mom, I did not want *their* food. Other mothers did weird things to their food. Mystery spices, green things, and dishes I straight-up did not recognize—no thank you. I'd make a beeline to the bowl I recognized from home. I'd get the potatoes or possibly some casserole, and then the tiniest bit of ham I could get away with. After that, it was cookie time.

Just one cookie on my plate, to start. Then the waiting game began.

In our church, the kids were allowed to get second helpings only after everyone had been through the line. You see the flaw in this reasoning. Everyone, yes, *everyone* would get to walk right by the cookies! How would they *not* take one? Without their moms hawk-watching them, they might even take two or three cookies! We would sit on the edges of our folding chairs, the entire youth group, staring at the cookies, willing hungry parishioners away from them. Sometimes it worked. Extra cookies! What could be better?

Only one thing: a potluck with *weapons*.

The absolute best kind of potluck dinner was the kind that followed a visit from a traveling missionary. On such occasions, a table in the back of the sanctuary featured all manner of foreign finds. Bowls, cups, clothing, and musical instruments—all clearly from somewhere very, very far away. This was fascinating stuff, but it couldn't hold a wick-in-a-bowl-of-oil candle to the weapons.

For some reason, visiting missionaries would often demonstrate the foreignness of their mission fields by bringing weapons from their mission fields. So the potluck tables would feature an array of homemade hatchets, slings, and arrows of all types for people to observe as they filled their plates. But the best part? Actual spears, displayed on the table you had just set up! *Spears!*

You get to see real-life spears and *then* eat a store-bought cookie? Man, it did not get much better than that.

# 7

# TV and Me

Once I turned 11, I would be placed in charge of the youth group members now and then when Mom and Dad weren't available. The rest of the youth group (i.e., my brother and sister) took that news like this:

My brother, Damon, two years younger than I: Did not notice or care.

My sister, DeeAnn, six years younger: "YOU'RE NOT THE BOSS OF ME!"

The easiest/best time for me to be in charge was from right after school until dinner. That's when the reruns played on our local TV channel.

There used to only be three TV networks. Now, there are more than 26,000. In fact, *you* very well may have your own TV network. Check your local listings.

But when there were only three networks, you could watch soap operas and game shows in the afternoon. That was it. If the price wasn't right, you were young and restless—unless you lived in or near a town large enough to have the vaunted "local channel." This wondrous enterprise would televise local baseball games or other events of local interest. And a tremendous number of reruns.

"Watch" is a loose, casual, and fun-sounding word for what the three of us would do. In reality, we would *study* the shows, fascinated by the goings-on, the hijinks, the tomfoolery, and the what-not. Especially the what-not. We watched TV in a silence that monks would envy. The telephone was ignored. The doorbell? It may as well not have existed. And only the most cogent, insightful comments were grudgingly allowed.

We typically watched the following programs:

A hilarious comedy about World War II, specifically, a prisoner of war camp. We had no idea what a prisoner of war camp was, or why it might not be the best setting for comic situations. We laughed when the Uber-Whatevers received their comic comeuppances, and we practiced our British accents because the British guy was the coolest.

A gentler comedy set, perhaps, in one of the Carolinas or Virginias? It was about a sheriff who rarely had to fight crime, but he did have to fight the temptation to eat a pie that was being saved for a special occasion. There was a regular character who was clearly a last-leg alcoholic. He literally locked himself in a jail cell to sleep off a bender.

A show about economics and extended family dynamics and the banking industry. Apparently, a man was planning to kill and eat something. This effort to stave off starvation resulted in an oil windfall. Another man, with a very thin mustache, tried to cheat the hunter out of his fortune, bit by bit. Two adult cousins and a senior citizen rounded out the family. The girl cousin often wore a shirt that she tied up so you could see some midriff drifting by.

Another group fought off starvation, this time on a deserted island. The two who should have been working on making some kind of boat would instead spend large parts of the day hitting each other with their hats while an elderly couple made faces. One woman wore a gown and another tied *her* shirt up. Must have been a thing back then.

An astronaut had his own genie, but he never, ever, wanted her to grant wishes. His best friend, also an astronaut, wanted to use wishes. Their boss, too old to be an astronaut, would often show up and puff out his cheeks in frustration and anger. There was no tied-up shirt in this one. Instead, the genie wore a top that never met her pajama bottoms. For some reason, this was a big deal, this rib-exposing. The scandal was mostly lost on us. But still.

And finally, the show that was, and still is, the best: A man worked on writing a TV show for another man, who was crazy. The writer's partners were a man who made jokes and a woman who was also funny. It was set in a suburb of New York, which was mysterious and glamourous. The lead male had a kid our age, and his wife did not need to tie up her shirt for us to get what he saw in her. I was watching the writers more closely than I knew.

# 8

# Skating By

The times our church had enough kids to constitute an actual youth group were memorable, because we finally got to do youth group things. I had imagined what this would be like, but I was way off. Even my wildest guesses never involved *skating*.

Be it skating on ice or on surprisingly hard and slightly banked wood, I never mastered this activity. I never got okay at skating. I never even got past being scared of skating, my fear sometimes approaching panic. But whoever was writing books about what to do with youth groups at the time was very big on skating, so the willing volunteers who had not been able to get out of volunteer duty were always taking kids skating.

For me, roller rink vs. frozen pond was basically a choice between two different ways to end up in the emergency room. You could fall on the wood or you could fall on the ice, but you *were* going to fall. The rink was full of kids who had some kind of different DNA and could skate backward easier than I could lace my rented death traps. On the ice, graceful pre-Olympians carved perfect figure eights until one apologetic kid with no apparent control of his limbs crashed into them. By comparison, even bowling was better.

But, wow, was I awful at bowling too. Like most preteen boys, I grew at a rate of about four inches a day. Subsequently, none of my clothes fit. I could outgrow a pair of jeans while trying them on. In short, I had an awkward phase that lasted more than a decade. It was not uncommon for me to fall while walking *up* the stairs. This made propelling a ball that weighed a tenth of my body weight down a straight path to the waiting pins a dicey proposition at best.

I would stand at the end of the alley, holding the ball in an approximation of what I saw around me. I summoned calm and courage that never came. Then I'd stumble forward and release the ball in a way that made it seem like the ball had suddenly escaped my hands.

I was no stranger to the gutter. I didn't even learn to keep score. Years later, I took bowling in high school gym class and got no better. But it could have been worse. It could have been swimming.

Three different times I took swimming lessons. And that's in addition to my dad trying to teach me on vacations or whenever we ended up at a pool. He'd dive off the diving board and swim to me, shivering in the shallow end. He would hold me horizontally while I kicked and windmilled my arms.

I also remember a nice lady at a lake who told my brother and me that we were not allowed to wear our just-bought masks into the lake. She also said something about going under and coming back up with a rock.

So, after failing at skating, bowling, and swimming, what's a kid to do?

Agriculture, perhaps?

# 9

# Lil' Emergency Room

My brother, Damon, is two years younger than I, and my sister, Dee-Ann, was six years younger, so she was mostly an irritant. To be fair, my brother was irritating too—but now and then, because cable TV hadn't been invented, we would play together.

We had Hot Wheels, and we'd put the tracks together and loop the loop and do all the stuff you can possibly do with very small stylized cars. We also had Tonka trucks that were indestructible. (I know this because I tried to destruct them often.) We did all the traditional stuff kids do, but one event stands out. Mostly because of the blood.

It was a Sunday afternoon. My brother and I were outside playing with our Lil' Gardeners set. Marketers and the greater grown-up infrastructure used to put the word *lil'* in front of things to get kids comfortable with the idea of working at thankless, heartbreaking jobs. Like farming.

So my brother and I were outside with our tools, which included (I'm not making this up) a solid steel hoe, a solid steel rake, and a solid steel shovel, all kid-sized. Unclear on even the most basic principles of farming, we quickly reverted to sword fighting. Sword fighting is the default activity of all boys everywhere when given one or two free minutes without adult supervision. Of course, you don't need an actual sword. Anything can become a combat weapon: yardsticks, brooms, or flyswatters—it doesn't matter.

The important question is, "Can I swing it at my brother's head, which is *right there*, a target my parents have graciously provided?"

My brother and I sword fought with the tools for a while. Then one of us struck on a brilliant idea. Specifically, if you threw the hoe into the big backyard tree, it stayed up there! Genius! Now there was a hoe in a tree, as nature intended. Next up? The rake. We lofted it treeward and voilà!

It stuck too. Now the steel hoe and the steel rake were swaying in the branches above. The shovel absolutely had to be next, right? Up it went.

Take a moment and visualize, if you will: A common, Lil' Gardeners–variety hoe has a built-in 90-degree angle. Therefore, if you throw it into a tree full of branches, it's probably going to find a home among those branches. That's just science. The rake boasts, perhaps, a 45-degree angle. Likewise, if you throw it in tree branches, it's going to stick.

Now picture the lil' shovel, with its zero-degree angle. It's just a blade. Made of steel. Shovel goes up. Shovel comes straight back down. And it's comin' fast.

Fortunately, I stopped the shovel with my head. It hit me right along the hairline, and, suddenly, I was Carrie at the prom. Head wounds bleed a lot. You can know that intellectually, but trust me, when it happens to you, it seems worse. I looked as if I'd pulled a red ski mask over my face.

I ran for the back door and grabbed the handle. Locked! Why? We'll never know. So I had to knock. This brought my mom to the door, where she encountered her firstborn covered in blood. For some reason, she did not faint. Bless her. Many towels were ruined, and then my dad was summoned. (Have I mentioned Mom doesn't drive? Mom doesn't drive.) Soon, I was off to the hospital.

What happened next? I can't say because I have no memory of it. But that night we attended church because it was open, and Dad was in charge. One of the youth group kids pointed at my head and laughed. Children can be cruel. I reached up to my former hairline and discovered that the front part of my head had been shaved, and I'd received several stiches.

What happened next? I can't say because the shovel severed the memory cells. But as I brought my hand down from my stiches and thought about hats, it occurred to me that this little shovel mishap was nowhere near the scariest thing that had happened to young me.

Not even close.

I'd also been in a tornado.

. . . . . . . . . . . .

The tornado also happened on a Sunday afternoon. Does that mean something? I'm not sure, but if there was a clear message about Sunday afternoons, it was something along the lines of "Holy heads-up!" from above—because that's where the impending drama is coming from.

An important piece of context here: Preachers work hard. Preachers' wives work even harder (but at least they're not paid), so Sunday afternoon is almost always nap time for pastoral families like the Taylors.

Also, at this time in our nation's history, if you were not looking directly at the TV and lived near a large-enough city to have that city's weather be *your* personal weather, you had to just go outside and check to see what was up, meteorologically speaking. No TV on, no warning. That's the upshot here. We were all sleeping soundly, especially, one imagines, my sister, who was about four months away from being born.

Then a freight train went through the house, just like people are wont to say when they describe tornadoes. It woke me up. It woke my brother up. One minute, we were lying on our twin beds. The next moment, we were lying on our twin beds and looking up at open sky.

They never found our roof. Or our garage, for that matter.

Disturbed by this sudden and unexpected home renovation, my brother and I climbed under the aforementioned twin beds. Then the mattresses moved as if thrown aside, because they were being thrown aside by my dad, who put one of us under each arm and headed up the street, with my pregnant mom in tow.

Where did we go? What did we do next? I have no idea. My memory of the details has been blurred by a kind of detail-obscuring mercy. We had an apartment for a while. Having been spoiled by single-family dwelling, we called the apartment, "the noise house." We kids thought it was exotic and interesting to hear strangers walking over our heads at all hours. Our parents were not as taken with that development. In my memory, it didn't take long before we were back to a single house where we made our own noise, but again, my memory of the whole thing is kind of blurred.

Today, I'm glad to say that summer, and even summer storms, don't make me think about tornadoes.

Summer makes me think of camp. You can learn why in the next chapter.

# 10

# The Order of the Fork

Our nondenominational denomination was part of a larger, loose orga-nization of similar churches. We occasionally combined forces to support missionaries, Christian colleges, and camps. As a pastor, my dad was often called upon to lead various camp events. I'm told I attended camp since I was a baby.

When you attend camp as a leader's kid, it's a pretty sweet deal. Mom worked in the kitchen while Dad preached and taught and swam. Mean-while, I was swaddled and laid in a drawer in the big camp kitchen. I don't remember that, but I do remember being old enough to basically have the run of the place.

As a young kid, camp was idyllic. My brother and I dashed in and out of the kitchen with the screen door slamming behind us as we ran into the big common area between the cabins. We climbed into the raf-ters of those cabins and read the G-rated graffiti inscribed there. Later, we headed to the canteen with a handful of change. There were camp-fires and lightning bugs and shooting stars.

When I reached the fourth grade, I was old enough to attend a camp week of my own without my parents around. That was not idyllic at all.

. . . . . . . . . . . . .

Our Datsun B210 pulled into the camp's dusty drive, and fourth-grade Dan exited the car, armed with only a sleeping bag, a suitcase, and a Bible.

Suddenly, the ground shook, and a deep rumble seemed to bub-ble up from the core of the earth as a full-sized bus rolled up the drive. A bus! That bus was full of fourth graders, whom, I imagined, were all best friends and had been forever. For all I knew, they had all been born in the same hospital on the same day. That was the beginning of a bond that made them all one.

I was also *one*, but in the more literal sense of the word. I made friends as well as I roller-skated. So, for me, camp became an exercise in the killing of time until the ordeal ended. Time proved resilient.

A bell rang, and we were directed to the common area between the cabins. Was this the same bell I'd had the honor of ringing just a couple of years before? Were these the commons where my brother and I had formerly frolicked? Yes, but, in a very real sense, no. Not at all.

We fourth-grade boys got to choose our own bunks in one of the three cabins. The girls did the same on the other side of the commons. I had been to the cleverly named Pee-Wee Camp the year before, but it was much more supervised. This was the Wild West. At the blast of a whistle, you were supposed to run to the cabin you wanted and throw your bag on a bunk to claim it, Manifest Destiny–style.

The busload of buddies signaled each other in their own language, consisting of hand signals and words only they understood. They ran to a cabin as if it were preordained. What I did was more like slinking toward the farthest cabin, figuring it would have space for me. It was full. So was the middle one. That left one choice, and only a couple of beds were available. I threw my bag on a top bunk, climbed up after it, and began my death match with time until the camp was over.

The bell rang each morning, first to wake us up and then to announce breakfast. The dining hall seemed huge now, with extra folding chairs and tables set up to accommodate a full camp. Everyone started eating. Inevitably, one kid would not want to eat. He would claim homesickness and leave the dining room crying. Determined not to be that kid, I kept to myself and worked on my industrial eggs.

Then the singing started.

Have you ever heard the song "The Order of the Fork"? Sorry, I should have warned you ahead of time that I was about to mention this traumatic tune. If you are fortunate enough to be unfamiliar with it, let me lay it out for you.

The lyrics are deceptively simple: *The Order of the Fork, the Order of the Fork, we are, we are, we are, we are, the Order of the Fork.* That's it. Sounds harmless, doesn't it? But those slightly cultlike lyrics hide a dark secret.

A cadre of campers marched around the dining hall tables, chanting the above refrain. Then, as if on cue, they stopped behind an unsuspecting diner. The victim was instructed to rise. Then the chant changed to something even more diabolical. Specifically, *Fee, fi, fo, foo! We initiate you!*

Then the chosen kid got stabbed (playfully!) with forks. I don't think anyone died from it, probably. I'm pretty sure it was "all in good fun," which is what people say when they fear a lawsuit.

I just knew I did *not* want to be initiated. I also knew I did not want to be *uninitiated*. These were tricky social waters I was wading into.

You see, all the popular kids were getting fork-stabbed. It was a rite of passage into the group of cool kids. You immediately got to join them as they marched and sang. I wanted to be included, but I knew I would be very glad if I did not get stabbed. Later, I would feel a little sad about *not* getting stabbed.

As I said, tricky social waters.

My years of recon (prior to reaching official camper age) had given me a working knowledge of the ins and outs of all the buildings. So, when I saw the Order of the Fork beginning to organize, I snuck out of the dining hall—a simple and elegant solution to an imaginary problem.

There was also a lot of time for Bible study at camp. Bible study at camp worked like this: You'd go off by yourself, just you and whatever bugs you attracted, along with your Bible and a pencil and single sheet of mimeographed lesson. You'd read whatever the lesson was about, generally how to be a better you. Then you'd read the assigned Bible passage and fill in a few blanks on your mimeographed sheet, thus demonstrating your mastery of a vital biblical concept.

Example:

God wants us to be good.

(Fill in the blanks) God wants __ to be ____.

Completing the day's assignment took about three minutes. They gave us half an hour. This freed up a lot of time, and as I moved from fourth grade toward the turbulent terrain of middle school, my thoughts turned, as you might have guessed, to girls.

And there were always lots of girls at nondenominational church camp.

# 11

# Dating in the Wild

Some religious traditions are strict about dating people only within one's tradition. But when your church is a self-proclaimed non-denomination, the process gets a little murkier.

Nondenominations had to let you in on the dating dos and don'ts only by hinting at them. Without bishops or sergeants-at-arms or whatever it is the actual denominations had, we were on our own. Preachers could preach and teachers could teach, but nobody was making policy at Nondenomination Headquarters (which was nonexistent). Each church was independent. The only rulebook we shared was the Bible.

There were specific things we were urged to avoid, of course. When we were really young, so young that cigarette commercials were still on TV, we were supposed to avoid cigarette commercials on TV. When those commercials came on, we would literally turn our backs on the TV. (DVR technology was pure science fiction back then. We couldn't simply fast-forward past the Marlboro Man.) Cigarette or alcohol commercials were not to be tolerated, no matter how catchy the jingle.

Maybe it worked, because none of us Taylor kids ever smoked. But I would eventually date a couple of girls who did, so I guess no system is perfect.

There are no Bible verses about smoking. And there are also no Bible verses about whether someone from the First Church of Something can or cannot date someone from the First Church of Something Else. I was never told that I could *not* date a girl from another church, but it wasn't encouraged. I certainly picked up on that. Girls from within our tradition? That was encouraged, so I picked up on *them*.

See what I did there, with the "picked up" phrase? That was much smoother than Middle School Me. As you saw in the previous chapter,

Middle School Me was not very smooth. But when your youth group is just your siblings, and you're at a camp that's full of girls who go to your same type of church, just in different towns, well, you don't have to be very smooth to at least *try*.

The place you tried was campfire. You asked a girl if she would "go to campfire" with you. Everyone was going. You had to go. This was the human equivalent of a lemming asking another lemming, "Do you want to tumble off the cliff?" But whether by choice or mandate, you and the girl could walk next to each other *in the dark*, which was key. Then you could sit together on hay bales that circled a large fire. (At least, it was large by city-kid standards.)

We did not have fires in the suburbs. Well, we did, but they were, you know, horrible accidents. Firetrucks came and extinguished them. Our leaves got raked and bagged, not torched. Usually, fires happened only in fireplaces. So a big ol' blaze outdoors was a big ol' deal. Pretty romantic stuff.

You sat there with your intended, even if you were unclear on what your intentions were. You sang songs, one of which was about a spark and fire, which seems a little on-the-nose now that I think about it. Then you heard *another* devotion because you hadn't heard one for almost six hours. Finally, it was time to trudge back toward the cabins. This was the moment of truth.

Your hands naturally hang at your sides when you're walking—unless you're in the jungle and have to clear the underbrush to move forward. Our camp was in the woods, but the path to and from campfire was probably 12 feet across and as clear as a front yard. So, hands at sides.

I'm right handed, so I wanted the girl on that side, with her hand hanging near mine. I would bump that hand, her left, with my right. I could claim it was an accident. I could say I was swatting a mosquito. I could wave the whole thing off if I had to.

Or, wonder of wonders, she could also "accidentally" bump her hand against mine, and *boom*! Sparks. (Even though sparks don't make a *boom* sound.) As the campfire song indicates (albeit in a different context), it only takes a spark and...*boom*!

Now we were holding hands.

Clearly, I had a girlfriend.

We were "going out." We were a "couple."

Romance at this age is mostly about language. Neither of us could drive, and we would be returning to our respective hometowns on Saturday morning. Had we exchanged addresses? Maybe. Would we write each other? Definitely not. Camp romances lasted only a week, and it usually took a couple of campfires to muster the nerve to reach for a hand. So we were looking at a three- or four-day deal, tops.

Camp romances are the mayflies of relationships, but they're important because they teach you valuable stuff about whose hand you want to hold and how to go about it. This would prove valuable to me eventually, but the path, while recently mowed, was still bumpy.

. . . . . . . . . . . .

At camp the summer between eighth and ninth grade, I went out with a girl we will call Beth to protect her anonymity—and because I can't remember her name. It's blocked out like a traffic accident you drive by and pray for the people involved. But you don't want to look directly at it.

Having graduated from just holding hands, I was now ready for the "putting the arm around her" move. This, of course, was a classic drive-in movie move, which could be employed even by those of us who could not drive yet.

Let's set the scene: The singing had ended, and the devotional message had begun. They were called "devotions" because it seemed a little too grand to call it a sermon, even though the principles were certainly there. The difference between devotions and sermons are mostly about setting. If you're sitting in a pew, it's a sermon. If you're sitting on hay bales, it's a devotion.

Devotions at camp had to last 15 minutes minimum. They usually ran for 20—sometimes up to half an hour. That gave a guy plenty of time to work if he was focused and had a plan. I was focused. I had a plan. My trusty right arm was practically touching Beth already. It would be a small thing to lift it, slip it around her shoulders, and pull her a little bit closer—but not *too* close.

Did I mention it was very dark? It was very dark, and of course I didn't want to look right at Beth. I wanted it to be more like, "Oh, this arm? This old thing? How'd it get there?"

So I was looking into the fire, which made me kind of blind. I began to swing my elbow in an arc that was intended to go behind her. And it would have—if it hadn't hit her right in the eye.

You know how people will say they're either a lover or a fighter? I was neither. Clearly not a lover, that's for sure, but not much of a fighter either. After all, I had just hit an innocent girl who had agreed to go to campfire with me. Beth crumpled on the hay bale. Her friends (middle school girls always travel with a phalanx of friends) stared daggers at me and comforted her as she began to cry. The guy doing devotions, I'm glad to report, never noticed anything.

I apologized all the way back to the cabins. I apologized to Beth, to her friends, to anyone who had witnessed the tragedy. Beth was pretty cool about it. If we had ever seen each other again, we might have laughed about it. But Saturday came and everyone had to go home. Beth and I promised to write, but, as previously noted, I am not even sure her name was Beth.

I can still clearly remember the shiner beneath her left eye, though, when we sat down to breakfast in the dining hall the next day.

My only consolation is that neither of us was initiated into the Order of the Fork.

# 12

# The Guy with the Guitar

During my church camp years, I was impressed by the enduring coolness of the Guy with the Guitar.

Sitting in the open-air chapel, TGWTG would walk onto the stage and just stand there. A hush would fall over the assembled. He would begin to strum, and people were transfixed.

One moment, we were swatting mosquitos and trying to get comfortable while sitting on the weedy ground in our shorts. Suddenly, along came TGWTG, and it was easy to pay attention.

TGWTG shined brightest at the campfire services. Like the kindling and the hay bales and the romantic tension, he was woven into the DNA of campfire. An argument could be made that TGWTG *made* the event. Without him, it would have been just a bunch of sticks meeting their collective fate.

And TGWTG wasn't just a big part of camp. He was a big part of nearly *every* youth group event. He *made* the event. Once he and his guitar got going...well, it only takes a spark.

. . . . . . . . . . .

Needless to say (which is what we utter right before going ahead and saying something), I wanted to learn how to play guitar. I was certain that I should, that I could, and that I would.

I took guitar lessons three different times. And like swimming, it never took. In a classroom setting, at a guitar store, and at home, I failed until I quit. I faked it until I didn't make it. Failure always came at the same point.

The D7 chord was my nemesis. Here's how you play the D7: You take three fingers and put them in precise spots on the neck of the guitar.

Then you strum with your other hand, and it sounds like a heavy object falling down carpeted stairs with thick foam padding. At least that's how it sounded every time I tried to play it. Unfortunately, there is no song that has a heavy object falling down stairs as part of it. Except maybe electronic dance music. (I don't think anyone knows how electronic dance music is made.)

My three failed attempts were separated by enough time that I'd forget how awful I was and hope would spring anew, as hope does. Between the second total fail and the third, I had somehow acquired a Led Zeppelin record I was not supposed to listen to.

I wasn't supposed to listen to it because of the loose-at-best moral ideas being set to music, but it turned out there was another very good reason not to listen. I was never, ever, going to be as good as Jimmy Page at guitar playing, no matter what. I understand now that no one *else* was going to be that good either. This was the musical equivalent of being introduced to basketball and thinking, perhaps with some practice, you'll be Michael Jordan.

But at the time, I'd go to a guitar lesson and then head home. I'd put my one "worldly" record on the turntable and listen to the soundtrack of my heart breaking. I could not make one chord sound like it was intentional. I would consider the onslaught of notes and chords involved in a song, and that was that. I was never going to be TGWTG.

I was okay with this realization. Not everybody needs to be onstage— or at the center of the campfire circle. Somebody needs to sit there and appreciate the music. And I did, because I knew a little bit about how impossible it was to play.

Years later, I made one last-ditch effort with an electric bass I borrowed from a friend, reasoning that four strings had to be easier than six. That turned out to not be the case, which is why I also never became the Guy with the Bass.

# 13

# Rock and Soul

That lone Led Zeppelin record I noted in the previous chapter was a bigger deal than one vinyl disc should be. The theology of rock music was a battle played out on my parents' furniture-sized stereo console and myriad 8-track and cassette players over the years. For most of middle school and all of high school, we were part of churches big enough to have youth groups and, therefore, official youth ministers. And some of these guys did not want to rock. Like, at all.

There were bands that played up a kind of theatrical spookiness that was easy to spot and easy to rule out. I was never going to be on a musical "Highway to Hell"—that was for sure. It was no big deal to avoid any and all Black Sabbaths, for example. But I was curious about the alleged "backward masking" on various rock records because it sounded like an interesting thing.

*Egassem drawkcab a s'ereht dik a llet reven.* That's "Never tell a kid there's a backward message," backward. See how interesting it is? Apparently, you needed a super fancy reel-to-reel system to play a whole song backward, but we tried with the turntable. It's a good way to break a phonograph needle, but we never heard any spooky messages. And throughout the experiment, I comforted myself with the knowledge that it wasn't my turntable, wasn't my album, wasn't my basement my friends and I were experimenting in.

Some youth leaders said we should just say no to the radio entirely. Not only the Captain, but also Tennille. These same leaders were not big on movies, especially once the rating system came into play and there was such a thing as *R*.

Today, looking at this issue from a parental viewpoint, I can see the problem more clearly. Lots of rock music was not what we'd call "God honoring." It wasn't meant to be, and some of it went to great lengths to make that clear. Lots of movies were the same way.

However, was the Rat Pack any better? Hard to say. They wore suits, and they didn't sing bad things, but what do we suppose actually happened on that "Slow Boat to China"?

Just as some youth group leaders were trying to slam the door on rock music as a genre, others were beginning to promote something called "Christian rock." Same drums, same guitars, same strained vocals, same D7 chords—but with a very different message.

I had friends who swallowed this genre hook, line, and amplifier. They bought albums, then 8-tracks, then cassettes, then CDs. They went to concerts, they wore the T-shirts, and they put the bands' stickers on their school notebooks.

Fortunately, my parents were big on the "pick your battles" principle. They never made any rules about music one way or another. So I went back and forth, sometimes swearing off (and once even throwing out) some rock albums—albums worth a *lot* of money now, just sayin'. Other times, I listened to rock albums and even attended a few concerts. But I always felt a little guilty about it.

Finally, I settled on a small collection of albums and 8-track tapes, which I looked forward to playing in my car.

Once I had a car—and a license to drive it.

# 14

# Driver's Dread

Remember driver's ed? I know that things have changed since I was a teen, but here's how it worked back then. If you lived on a farm, you started driving around nine years old. The surly but good-hearted sheriff recognized your family pickup, and he didn't mind *not* seeing a head through the windshield. He simply assumed that yet another eight-year-old had turned nine and was now driving around, attending to official farm business. Cool.

This scenario might seem dangerous and far-fetched, but I know it's true, because my wife, Lana, lived it. She could drive a stick shift by the time she was ten.

However, for us city kids, you had to pass a driver's education class before you could take the test to earn your license. And you couldn't be nine years old. We city kids hit the road seven years after our country counterparts.

Typically, the driver's ed instructor was a teacher who had lived a full life and was ready to meet whatever lay beyond this world. That's why these teachers evoked a kind of otherworldly calm. They would sit in the passenger's seat (with an aftermarket brake pedal added) and guide their neophyte charges through the rigors of the road.

My driver's education teacher sat in the front seat, reading a newspaper, and occasionally muttering, "Turn left at the next street."

Basically, that was the extent of his guidance. "Turn left. Turn right."

We did have to do a few drills. One of these involved keeping the car's speed at a steady 35 mph.

Other times, a series of turns would bring me to a specific destination, like the hardware store. Then the teacher would say, "Wait here," before he went inside to buy some stuff.

Then it was another series of turns, and we arrived at a donut shop.

"Wait here," he'd say again. He would return with donuts. (For him, *not* for the kids in the car.) Then it was back to school.

This was the routine for several weeks. Then the "class" was over because you had learned to drive. I could have also put quote marks around the words *learned* and *drive* in the previous sentence, but that would have been too many quote marks, and I think you get my point.

For me and my fellow students, driver's education class meant trips to the dry cleaners, various grocery and houseware stores, and, of course, the donut shop. Our teacher basically had a team of chauffeurs at his service.

One of those chauffeurs was a girl.

I tried to impress that girl. Really tried. With my excellent driving, with my perfectly timed, "Can you believe we're getting donuts again?" eye rolls, and by simply trying to be very, very cool. Or so I imagined.

None of that worked for me. When the class ended, so did the potential love connection. It didn't matter, though, because I had another option ready. On the first Friday after I got my license, I was ready for a "car date."

It's important to note some architecture here. At the time, my family lived in a house that, duplex-style, shared a central wall with the identical adjoining house. There were no other duplexes in the neighborhood. I don't think there were any others in the town, but for some reason this was two houses stuck together on one slightly larger than normal lot. For that reason, the driveway for each house ran down the side of the house, heading to a freestanding four-car garage in back. Two spaces for us, two for our neighbors.

This meant, as you can probably see in your mind because of my detailed technical description, you had to make a pretty severe turn to get lined up for the garage once you cleared the house.

This is why, on my third day as a licensed driver on his way to his first car date, I hit my own house with my dad's car. I scraped and "lightly dented" the entire passenger side of the car. The side my date was going to see.

Dad was surprisingly cool about it, but he did suggest that maybe I should start looking for my own car.

I agreed, not so much because I felt bad about damaging his car, but because his car didn't even have an 8-track player.

# 15

# Speaking of Speakers

My first car was a 1967 Dodge Coronet 440. Not the cool kind of Coronet. Oh, they're classics now, coveted American muscle cars. Mine was just old, but that didn't matter. It was mine.

My grandfathers were a mailman and a mechanic. By the time I was born, the mailman was retired, and, while his encyclopedic knowledge of zip codes was impressive, it didn't do me much good.

My other grandpa, on the other hand, found me my first car. This was long before cars came with computers, and even before "diagnostics" were a thing mechanics did to see why your car was making that noise. In other words, a guy who knew what he was doing could find a used car, check it out, and decide whether it would be a good, reliable deal or not.

I was *not* a guy who knew what he was doing. My dad wasn't either. Fortunately, Grandpa was, and he found a maroon 440 for $350. That's right, 350 American dollars. About what you'd spend today for custom laser-cut rubber floor mats.

When you make $2.94 an hour working after school at a grocery store, $350 for a car is about right. I bought my car with cash. I paid for my own gas and the occasional oil change. But my car needed something else, something else that would cost money.

Better speakers. Obviously.

Speakers were the currency of a high schooler's self-bought car. The Novas, the giant Buicks, the beat-up trucks—they were all about the same level of okay. "It starts up" was the baseline of the automotive experience. It was also the apex of the automotive experience.

But the speakers? That's where differentiation was everything. Unfortunately, I couldn't afford a deluxe sound system when I was making $2.94 an hour. And if I had asked my parents for money for car speakers for a vehicle that already *had* speakers…well, I can see their mystified looks right now.

It took around 30 hard-earned dollars for a pair of speakers that were *maybe* slightly better than the ones that came with the car. Further, that massive cash outlay provided just two speakers and a bunch of mystery wire. Bluetooth was just a weird disease back then—or maybe the name of a pirate. If you wanted speakers, you needed miles of wires.

So I had the speakers and the wires. Now what? Fortunately, my "sound system" came with a single page of indecipherable instructions. I spent countless hours with my awkward six-foot body sprawled across the front floorboards, trying to discern what went where.

For example, old cars like mine had a ledge behind the back seat, rather like a windowsill. The ledge was a much-desired feature in cars at that time. On long car trips, my parents would put a pillow and blanket up there, and it served as a loft for my sister. If parents placed a kid on the ledge today, they'd be hauled off to federal prison for the rest of their wayward lives. But back then, riding the ledge was standard operating procedure.

The backseat ledge was made out of some kind of pressboard. As previously noted, my dad was not what you'd call a handyman, so he was of no help in the speaker installation process. That's how I found myself on my knees in the back seat, facing the rear window with a steak knife and a dream.

It's difficult to plunge a steak knife into your car without a degree of self-doubt. And it should be. I shudder to think what kind of person would gleefully do such a thing. With fear and trembling, I cut two holes into the car. I hoped those holes would match the size of my aftermarket speakers.

They did. The speakers worked, and a few short hours later, I was ready to hit the road, rockin'. And I did just that for about three days. That's when I noticed the strange rattling sound. Not to get overly technical, but speakers come with cones. These cones tear if you use the speakers. Then you have to take the raspy speaker apart and tape the cone. That usually fixes the problem—until you decide you might want to use the speaker again. So I ended up with the kind of speaker system a kid making $2.94 an hour deserved.

Rattling rockin' is still rockin', though, so it was all right with me.

# 16

# Early Works

The grocery store job that supplied me with a car, speakers, replacement speakers, and gas to drive around for no reason whatsoever was not my first job. My first job was at a ladies' dress store. Jealous? Um, you really should not be. It was not much of a job, but at least the pay was low.

The best thing about making zero dollars an hour is that it makes *any* dollars an hour sound like a pretty good deal. I don't remember what I made at the ladies' store. I don't even remember the name of the ladies' dress store. Coronet Junior Beehive sticks in my memory, but that makes no sense. Not surprisingly, it didn't produce any results in my recent Google search either.

Every other day after school, I would walk to the mall where the store sat amid other stores I can't remember and a bank. I remember the bank because I got to carry a zipper pouch of money there every time I worked. This struck me as a big responsibility, and I took it very seriously. Looking back, however, it's easy to see that I was regarded as the dress shop's most expendable staff member. If anyone was going to get mugged en route to the bank, my bosses determined it should be me.

In addition to the banking, I was also in charge of vacuuming. The store was 100 percent carpet. I don't mean to brag, but that was a pretty big deal. Emptying trash was another high-priority task for me. Also, on rare occasions, I got to disassemble, move, and rebuild the round racks that displayed the sweaters.

The most demanding part of the job, though, was getting bags out of the attic. The attic was about four feet tall. I was about six feet tall. So I'd hunchback around in the near dark, looking for bags the salespeople called by what seemed to me to be arcane nicknames.

For example, they'd be out of 16s. I had to go up and get lots more 16s.

How many? "All of them!" they'd say. The problem, of course, was that the 16s were gone, so there was no template for me to follow. I learned this by bringing down a healthy supply of 24s.

I don't know what you know about bags, but 24s…well, they are not 16s. Not by a long shot.

So it was back into the attic. I returned with what, even to me, did not look it could possibly be anyone's idea of a 16. I was right. It was wrong.

So it was back to the attic again. I kept at it until I literally stumbled on the 16s. I brought them all down, and that's when we ran out of 54s. Do you know what 54s look like? Neither did I.

My dress shop job would have been pretty terrible if not for one thing. My girlfriend lived near the mall. At a predetermined time each workday, she would head for the long cinder-block wall that formed the back of the mall. That wall was perforated by one metal door per business, and when you got let in (there was no way to open them from the outside), you found yourself in an indoor alley between the parking lot and the back of each business. This is, as it turns out, a pretty romantic spot when you're 14. Nothing seems as awesome as kissing while seated on a big stack of 54s.

# 17

# Sports, Part 1

Some preachers establish a dynasty and stay at one church for decades. They become fixtures in their towns, revered by the other churches and even the school board. They pray before town council meetings, that kind of thing. Others move every few years, either at the behest of a ruling body or because they just do. My dad was the second kind of preacher.

I was the "new kid" more times than I'd like to remember, so I'd employ various strategies to overcome any attendant awkwardness.

None of the strategies worked. My attendant awkwardness had perfect attendance. Two of my biggest strategic failures happened at two different high schools.

At the first school, I thought I'd go out for cross-country. There's a hint in the name as to what's horrible about cross-country. You are going to run a long way. Even in a small country this would be true, much less one that ranges from one shining sea to another.

What made a kid who could neither roller- nor ice-skate, swim, or hit anything but the most generously lobbed softball think about sports? I have no idea. And of all sports, why one of the most physically demanding? Again, no idea, but there was plenty of time to ponder as I pounded the pavement.

I ran three miles every morning before school and three more miles after school. If that doesn't sound like a lot to you, then we will probably never be close. I was about 6 feet tall and weighed maybe 140 pounds. At a glance, there wasn't much that precluded me from becoming a runner. Nothing but a staggering lack of will, drive, determination, and other things coaches talk about. The main thing staggering was me. During practice, I'd focus on an upcoming telephone pole or mailbox and literally flop one foot in front of the other until I got there. Warmed on the inside by this speck of success, I'd choose another nearby goal.

About three weeks into the three-mile, twice-daily regimen, Mom and Dad announced we were moving. No teen was ever so glad to be uprooted.

Soon, it was a new school but the same old struggle to be "one of the guys." Specifically, one of the guys who did not drink or swear or get high. Further, I was one of those guys who was, as we said in church, "saving myself for marriage." (Nobody ever admits it, but this self-saving is much, much easier when no one is asking you.)

I still could not skate, swim, bat, shoot, or kick. And I had recently learned that I could not run either.

So I decided to try wrestling.

If you know anything about wresting, you're laughing at me already. You know what? I don't blame you. That is a cool-headed assessment of my prospects in the sport of wrestling. And if you want to keep laughing, consider this: I joined the wrestling team to meet girls.

Oh, you may laugh, but there were girls involved in the wrestling program at this school. They were charmingly called the Mat Maids. They did things like roll up the mats and lug them to storage after practice. *I* wasn't strong enough to do that.

I wrestled for about as long as I ran cross-country. Every day I took salt tablets to ward off dehydration during practice. Every day I consulted with my parents to see if we could move again. Because I hated wrestling. Every day we did endless drills. One of these involved balancing yourself on the back of a teammate and spinning as fast as you could with your stomach on his arched back and then trading places. That's exactly as fun as it sounds.

I could have wrestled at 132. Not the time in the afternoon, but the weight. I was 6 feet tall and weighed 132 pounds. Are you familiar with the term "high center of gravity?" If so, you're laughing again. I *could* have wrestled at 132, but there was no spot on the team at 132 because some of the best wrestlers in the state were vying for that spot. There was serious talk about my dropping to 126 pounds, but I had already left the room and wrestling.

In fact, I started "forgetting my gym clothes" right up to the limit you could do this without failing gym class. When you forgot your gym clothes, you had to sit out with the stoners. Because I was not getting stoned, our conversation was limited. That was okay with me. I was just killing time until college. That's where I planned to come into my own.

As it turned out, I was not a very good planner.

# 18

# Bible College, Part 1

High school seniors face a series of big, life-altering decisions. That's too bad, because high school seniors are only 17 or 18 years old.

Some of these seniors are mature beyond their years. By the time he was a senior, my younger brother was clearly demonstrating the talent and dedication that would make him a successful commercial artist one day.

I, on the other hand, was not demonstrating any such talent, because I graduated high school with no recognizable career skills.

Math was a foreign language to me, and I was not good at foreign languages. Science was a universe of mystery, and not in the, "Hey, this is kind of interesting" way—like when you stumble on a PBS show about luminescent plants or something. I'm talking about the "I have no idea what you're talking about" kind of mystery.

Further, I was proving to be an unsuccessful youth group leader, at least in part because I could not skate or swim. I couldn't even play capture the flag competitively, much less lead a lesson or a chorus.

However, I did love God, and I believed church was where all manner of good things happened. And my dad, several of my uncles, and assorted other influencers in my life made it seem as if full-time Christian service was a good idea for me.

Where should I prepare myself for this service? Obviously, at the same Bible school that my dad, mom, and several of those aforementioned uncles attended.

That school offered various areas of study, leading to careers such as senior minster, youth minister, music minister, missionary, or future grad student.

None of those callings called to me, so I was cruising along under the "general studies" banner. Here, in bullet-point form, are the reasons I had to quit Bible college after one semester:

- I came to college from the suburbs of a large city. Most of the other students did not.

- I had very little in common with most of the students (see above).

- I did not have a favorite Christian recording artist, as everyone else did.

- I had a girlfriend at home.

- The whole thing reminded me of camp.

When people talk about God's plan for their lives, they nearly always do so in hindsight. There's even a poem about this. Perhaps you know it. It's the one about the tapestry. Right now, we can only see the rough side of the tapestry, but once we're in heaven, we will see that it's all part of God's beautiful plan. (This poem is available in poster form if you're looking for something to put on your walls.)

For me, Bible college (at least part 1 of Bible college) was all wrong-side-of-the-tapestry time. My hair was wrong, my clothes were wrong, and my hometown girlfriend was wrong. I couldn't sing. I couldn't learn Greek. (There's a reason "It's Greek to me" is a popular saying.) I couldn't pray out loud for more than a few sentences.

I was a fish out of water. There were three other fish like me at this school, and they were easy to spot. These students came from a different part of the big city than I did, but we had a lot in common. So we shared rides home on weekends and ate in the cafeteria together during the week. We were different together.

A single semester doesn't sound like a lot of time, but those days went slowly. In fact, the weekends I ended up stranded on campus were just straight-up glacial. No one was even a little bit surprised when, at the end of that first semester, I quit college and went home.

At the time, I wondered if I would ever be back.

# 19

# Failing at the Factory

Pioneers, visionaries, originators—they can come from anywhere, and often they don't even know they're breaking ground and blazing a trail.

I kind of invented the "Your adult kids will come back after you thought they had left for good" thing. Sorry, but that was me.

I'll explain. My parents didn't need to cajole me into finding a job right away. My empty pockets and empty hours cajoled themselves. But my parents were a big help on several jobs I secured and lost in quick succession. They also helped me find the one job that actually lasted for a short while.

Dad knew a guy who worked at a factory that made many things. I say "many things" because I really have no idea what the factory made, except for my little piece of it. My area was airplane parts. Scary, right? I was 19, and I had been demonstrating, across multiple platforms, that I could not competently do much. Apparently, this made me a great candidate for creating airplane piston pins.

Piston pins, as far as I could tell, were metal cylinders that came in various sizes. I didn't *actually* make them. That would have required skill and training. I just inspected them. To make sure they could go into planes. *Air*planes. Next time you're cruising at 30,000 feet, think about that.

I started on the day shift, which was where all the training took place. Then I would be assigned to one of three shifts. The inspection process was deceptively simple, so I was a perfect fit for it. I stood in a four-foot-square canvas tent that blocked out all ambient light. There was a black light, like they use at crime scenes. I poured a phosphorescent liquid on the piston pin, and this would make any imperfections show up clearly.

Then the real fun started! I would write down the details of the crack or chip or fissure—the length, depth, and width. Then I'd check a collection of encyclopedias for the admissible variances. "Wow, would computers have made a difference!" is probably what you're saying right now. But there weren't any at the time. Just a Smithsonian Institute's worth of notebooks.

Somehow, I completed my training. Somehow, they offered me a full-time, second-shift job. Somehow, I'd have to explain to my parents I was not taking the job. Why not? I was 19 years old! There was no way on God's green earth I was going to work 2:00 p.m. to 10:00 p.m. So I hinted to Mom and Dad I maybe had been mysteriously and inexplicably laid off after only three weeks of successful training. They knew better, but they also knew that airplane part inspecting was probably not the path laid out for me. There you go. Unemployed again.

But not for long! It's a shame you can't meet my dad. He's in heaven now, and I suppose he's met just about everyone and set up coffee times with all of them. He knew everybody on earth, so that wouldn't be a big challenge for him.

One of the guys he knew owned a vending machine company. Can you guess what happened next?

# 20

# Not the Correct Change

The next time you see a massive panel van next to you on the highway—and you notice that the guy driving it seems rather young and not too good at driving it—just be glad he's not inspecting airplane parts.

The vending machine business, at least in the late 1970s, worked like this: You got a truck and a map, and you took off to service your machines. An experienced guy would follow you in a pickup and go in to each stop and evaluate your vending-machine-stocking performance: "Dan did this well." "Dan messed up this one." Most of my critiques were the latter.

Day one at this job saw me driving a truck with a manual transmission. I had driven a stick car, but that's like saying, "My family used to have a terrier, so I can probably ride a camel." The route went through hill and dale. The dales were okay, but the hills were just awful.

At one point, as I tried to climb a downtown hill that came straight up from a river valley, I knew I had met my match. I put the truck in Park and got out. Right on the street. Then I waited for the guy following me in the pickup. He took over. After that, I drove only automatics.

You learn a lot about people when you're in the vending machine business. Most of what you learn is not very good. You know how you can sometimes get a dollar to work in a machine, while other times you might as well be using yen? There's a reason for that. Each machine has sensors that read a bill, and that bill must meet certain specifications. Your dollar doesn't have to be of just-minted quality, but it can't be a drawing you did at home. Somehow, the sensors on a dollar bill changer at one of my stops were off-kilter. This friendly machine was accepting photocopies of a dollar, providing candy, and giving back a dollar's worth of change. I know this because when I opened up the machine I found a giant stack of Xeroxed dollars and no change.

Another time, I entered the break room of an office and met a manager who was patiently standing by a machine with a broken lock. About half of the candy had been taken before he realized the problem.

One of my stops was always trouble. Years before I started, the company had crossed picket lines to fill the vending machines because the vending contract was with management, not labor. Say what you will about unions, they can hold a grudge. I'd find gum in the coin returns. Cans of soup would be ignored until they exploded in the machine from botulism or some other built-up toxins. And worst of all, no one would talk to me or even look at me. Even though I was nowhere near siding with management, I couldn't explain that to anyone. This added a level of social awkwardness that made a bad situation worse.

But my feelings really got hurt when I had to fill soda machines at a junior college. There's a certain look that one 19-year-old can give another. It says, "Hey! We're the same age, but you're stuck in a vending-machine job, and my options are as limitless as the endless horizon. My future is as bright as the dawn because I'm going to junior college and you're not!" That's when I decided I would try junior college. But not before the soda can incident.

A nearby town on my route had a slaughterhouse, where our company had a vending contract. The breakroom featured a soda machine that held lots of cans in a serpentine pattern. You paid your money, a lever released one can, and the rest of the cans rolled forward, ready to quench the next customer's thirst. Unless it got stuck.

To remedy this stuck-can situation, I thought it would be a good idea to reach into the opening where the cans came out and move the lever. So I did. It worked like a charm, and the cans rolled forward. That put the lever back where it used to be, except for my four fingers, which were now wedged between the lever and all the cans. It was a lot of cans. I was trapped up to my shoulder, looking a lot like a country veterinarian trying to deliver a calf.

Then break time started. The room filled with guys who had small swords on their belts and blood on their plastic aprons. Looking at these men, I became keenly aware of the 200 $1 bills in my pocket. At that point, I really wished the bills were just Xerox copies. The butchers took in the scene, laughed at me, and went back to their breaks, only without Cokes.

Fifteen minutes later, the guy who followed/evaluated me entered the room. He took one look and went back out to his pickup. He returned with the biggest screwdriver I've ever seen. He levered the cans off my hand, and we pledged to never speak of it again.

That's the day I decided on junior college, but I still had to work to pay my tuition.

And that's where baby trees entered the picture.

# 21

# A Nursery for Trees

Another guy in the endless line of guys my dad knew owned a tree nursery. They grew baby trees along with all kinds of plants and flowers and ground cover and sod. All this foliage needed watering. The nursery already employed a head waterer, but an assistant waterer was needed too. That's where I came in.

I'm a pretty good judge of ages, so when I tell you the head waterer was 100, perhaps even 120, you can be sure I'm close. The dude was very old; that's what I'm suggesting. Many of his teeth had already given up the fight, and this made it easier for him to chew tobacco all day. Keen to fit in, I tried smokeless tobacco. Turns out there's a trick to chewing tobacco. The trick is *never chew tobacco*. But if you do, don't swallow. I didn't know that, and I got very sick. It made me understand why those teeth did not want to be in that guy's mouth.

Assistant waterer may sound like a fancy job, but it was pretty easy to figure out. You walked around with a hose and watered things. It was kind of a dream job in some ways, one that probably doesn't exist anymore. Sprinklers do the bulk of the work now. I did not learn anything about plants as assistant waterer.

There were a couple of real perks to this job. I was as tanned as I'm ever going to be in my life, and I got to listen to music all day. To accomplish that second part, I took a battery-operated FM radio that was about the size of lunchbox and hooked the handle to a guitar strap (which was left over from the never learning to play). Then full-sized, over-the-ear headphones on a thick curling cord completed the look. High fidelity FM music delivered right to your eardrums for as long as the batteries lasted. Did the guitar strap mess up the tan? Of course it did. Small price to listen to music all day.

At this time, I was going to junior college and working 20 hours a week or so. An opportunity to do a better-paying job for yet another friend of my dad's came up, so I said *adios* to the tree nursery and began working construction.

And, with that, Bible college, part 2, was beginning to seem like a thing I might actually be able to afford. Someday.

# 22

# Drywall, Coffee, and No Beer

If you're not a construction worker, when you hear "construction worker" you probably go to one of two places in your mind. You think of a busy urban site where guys in hard hats shout inappropriate things to women who walk by. Or you think of a 1980s disco group that featured a construction worker, as well as a Native American, a police officer, and a cowboy.

The majority of construction jobs are much less confrontational (or musical). They are mostly just guys going to work at commercial or residential sites. The guy my dad knew worked on houses. So it was residential construction for me, and I can explain the entire job in one paragraph.

The two-by-four-inch wooden boards that make up the skeleton of a house need walls. Otherwise, wolves can get in. So four-by-eight-feet sheets of drywall are nailed or screwed onto those two-by-fours by guys who hang the boards in place. Such guys are called hangers. Then the seams between those boards need to be taped closed and smoothed over so the walls can be painted. The guys who tape those seams are called tapers. I was a taper.

Technically, I was only an assistant taper. (Apparently, I showed a real aptitude for assisting.) The guy I worked for would subcontract to tape the seams on a house. Once the hangers were done with the walls, we'd come in and put the tape on. See how simple that sounds?

It's not that simple.

My boss would take a tool we called a bazooka, because that was a cool-sounding name, and fill it with drywall mud. The bazooka was a tube that had a spool of drywall tape on the end of it. He would run the tape down the seam, dispensing a thin layer of mud and laying the tape right in the middle of it. He was an artist at this. It was a really impressive thing to see.

I got to be impressed a lot because my job was to follow behind with a pan and a drywall knife and "pull" the tape, which meant push it securely into the seam and clean up any excess mud.

We'd do this on every wall and ceiling in a house, finishing a two-story, 2,000-square-foot house in a couple of days. Then, another layer of mud went over the dried tape, and another layer over that. Sand it, and if things went well, you'd never see the seams once the walls and ceilings were painted.

I loved that job, and I was okay at it. The money was good, but there were problems. Those problems helped nudge me back to Bible college. Specifically…

- Pretty much every day, and especially Friday, ended with beer. At the time, I believed that good people did not drink beer.

- No old people were doing drywall. The only old people you'd see owned companies and ran several crews. You'd see them driving around in trucks and reading the paper. You would *not* see them carrying boards upstairs. This was not a career gig.

- I still wanted to do what I thought God wanted me to do, and this job didn't seem to be it.

- While I was a fine assistant who could pull tape like a pro, it became pretty clear that I was never going to get good at running the bazooka. Running the bazooka, like ice-skating, looked easy if you were good at it. I got to work on garages— terrible-looking garages. I'd run the gun the length of a ceiling, sometimes while wearing stilts(!). But while this looked super cool as it happened, the magic didn't last for me. The entire length of the ceiling's worth of tape would stay up there for few seconds, and then it would all fall down. On me. A muddy mess. I'd have to put it up there by hand, which took forever and never looked right. So my drywall days were limited.

- Finally, each day on the construction site began with a big cup of coffee. I was 20 and had never consumed coffee. But each day ended with beer, and I wasn't going to go that route. I determined I needed to do some kind of social drinking, and coffee seemed like the lesser of two evils. I decided to drink my coffee black, no sugar. This seemed like the toughest, baddest thing you could do with coffee, so that's what I did.

Today, I still drink my coffee black, although I am pretty sure it would be much better with some stuff in it.

# 23

# Bible College, Part 2

Convinced that the fields of airplane building, food vending, tree nursing, and home construction could get along without me (and after a year of junior college), I decided to throw myself back into Bible college.

When I returned to school, I found that little had changed. My handful of friends were quite a bit further along in their academic journeys. Some of them had become really good at Greek and were starting to learn Hebrew.

The friends who had advanced in biblical languages made me think maybe I could learn Greek. They did not make me think I could learn Hebrew, which was daunting guys I knew were much smarter than me...or is it I? See what I mean? But I thought I could figure out Greek, and with dedication, determination, and hours of study, I learned how to say, "The crowd hears a voice." Not bragging, but even now, if I were somewhere with a crowd of ancient Greeks, and there was a sound in the distance, and that sound was a voice, and someone asked me what the crowd heard, I could say, in their own language, "The crowd heard a voice." And that is the sum total of the Greek I know today. Sadly, it's just a little less than the total I knew while I was studying it.

I knew students who mastered both languages, and I knew professors who worked internationally on thorny translation issues. Those people, then and now, were as mysterious and impressive to me as magicians. I could make the Statue of Liberty disappear as easily as I could conjugate a simple Greek sentence. Fortunately, you only needed one semester of Greek to be a youth minister. Career path established!

# 24

# Sports, Part 2

At this Bible college, willing volunteers joined the soccer team rather than tried out for the soccer team. That's because our school had never before fielded a soccer team. There were no precedents, no moving stories of seasons past. And there were no coaches. The team was "coached" by a couple of older students who also played on the team. Many of us had never seen a soccer ball up close before. We had never stood on a soccer field, much less coaxed a ball down one without using our hands.

So if you could stand on the appointed field on the appointed day at the appointed time, you became a member of the soccer team. I had already proven my lack of prowess at running, and I had added the Freshman 15 to my frame, followed by the less alliterative (but still measurable) Sophomore 15. Thus, I was a natural to play defense.

But even if you're a defender, it turns out that soccer is mostly running. We have already established that I do not run well.

Fortunately, the prescribed path for post-practice runs followed a big oval around the baseball field and then past the equipment shed. The other guy who got assigned to play defense was just as born (not) to run as I was. We were always at the back of the pack. By a lot. By so much, in fact, that when we rounded the equipment shed we quickly noted that we were alone and could not be seen by the rest of the team. So we slumped against the shady side of the shed. We sat for a while and then lay on the grass and tried to make our lungs work. Once that was accomplished, we joined the rest of the team.

I never got better at running. I never got to a point where I looked back on those lazy days with scorn.

Also, our team never got very good at soccer. We never even got kind-of good. We might have approached just regular-level bad a couple of times, but that's being generous. Here are some ways we were beaten:

- A team beat us by more than 11 to 0. I still remember the score because every member of the opposing team scored a goal on us—including the goalie, who brought the ball from one end of the field to the other by himself.

- A "club" team beat us. We thought they'd be easy to beat because they were just a bunch of guys who met at a bar and decided to form a team. Plus, they were old, like 26. It turned out these guys had been playing together for more than a decade.

- A team that spoke a language none of us could recognize seemed to have a great time beating us, judging by their huge smiles and excited, indecipherable shouting.

- A team beat us before we ever got out of the vans by coming from an area where every field seemed to sprout soccer goals. We saw those fields for miles and miles and knew we were doomed.

Some of us had girlfriends who came to the games. That didn't help. The baseball team had cheerleaders. So did the basketball team. We had a scattering of disappointed girlfriends. There were no cheers to lead.

We had one win, and it was a qualified win at best. We were playing another Bible college, so there was a glimmer of hope. We were not losing by much when the sleet started. Freezing needles of rain came at us sideways, and we were wearing thin polyester shorts and shirts.

Halftime was held in the chapel, which was a huge building with classrooms and stuff. We huddled in a hallway and shivered. The other team opted not to come back out for the second half. Sensing technical victory, we took the field and won, frozen solid, by forfeit. This was decades before the "participation trophy" era, but in our hearts, we had trophies.

# 25

# Girlfriends

In middle school (which we called junior high) and high school, being the new kid brings one real advantage into the realm of romance. As the new guy, you emit this "grass is greener" vibe, as opposed to the boys the girls already know—know as knuckleheads, to be specific.

"Does this new kid also have a head full of knuckles?" the girls wonder. No one knew. This was good news for me, bad news for the local lads. Which sometimes turned into bad news for me after all. If you think local guys like it when a new kid is getting the attention they believe should belong to them, you don't know much about those local guys. It could be scary, and I learned to make myself scarce.

But the girls were still there, still somewhat interested in me. So what's a guy to do? I pretty much had a girlfriend, or was looking for one, from the age of 12. "Son of the preacher" was not a bad title. While my mom and dad didn't always enjoy "being under the microscope," my brother and I didn't mind being under scrutiny—as long as girls were the ones doing the scrutinizing.

Of course, romances at this age are mostly theoretical. You might be "going out" with a girl, but you were not actually going anywhere. As for displays of affection, holding hands was as far as it went. You talked *about* relationships much more than you actually participated in one.

Reaching driving age helped you elevate your game. You could go to a particular hut famous for its pizza. You attended a few movies, and, occasionally, collided with your love interest at the roller-skating rink.

Before I hit college age, a girl moved into the other side of the duplex in which we lived. She would be my girlfriend for almost two years. We were deliriously happy for weeks at a time, then deliriously unhappy (over who knows what) for equal intervals. She was the main reason I came home from college every weekend—either to break up or make up.

At one point, I decided I needed to be with her so much that I quit college and moved home. We broke up for good about one week later.

My mom was a college junior when she quit school to marry my dad, who had just graduated. I attended that same school, and 20 years later, not much had changed. The big campus joke about women seeking a "Mrs." degree still circulated, and it was still only half funny. This was a time when "pastor's wife" was still a viable career choice, and I was at a school full of guys planning to be pastors. After finishing my junior year as an unattached pastor-to-be, I was worried I would end up as the male version of an old maid.

Bible college students often got weekend jobs as youth ministers, and I was doing that each weekend—and working almost full-time during the summers. And summer youth-ministering meant camp.

I quickly discovered that being a camp counselor was much better than being a camper. No one could force me to swim or play softball. And "lights out" simply meant that it was time to hang out with the other leaders, staying up as late as we pleased.

Then, one Sunday evening, at this camp I'd been attending most of my life, everything changed.

Changed by one girl.

# 26

# The Last Girlfriend

Our church camp welcomed more than 100 campers during busy weeks, so organization was required. Campers were divided into groups, sometimes randomly, sometimes by school grade. One particular year, all high schoolers were divvied into groups called families.

I was the counselor for a group of ten kids, but like a pre-Eve Adam, there was no helper suitable for me. I sat my charges in a circle in the commons. We were about to start a rousing game of "two truths and a lie" or something else designed to build lifelong relationships. Then a van pulled into the dusty drive where I had been dropped off so many times, and the worship leaders for the week got out.

As one of them walked toward us, it occurred to me that this could be a much, much better week than I had anticipated.

She crossed the commons. She entered our circle and said, "I'm supposed to be here?" with a hint of a Southern accent and a ponytail on the side of her head. I thought, *Yes, you are definitely supposed to be here.*

. . . . . . . . . . . .

Camp counselor is a funny title. There are volunteers who are youth leaders in their home churches. And there are professional ministers, like my dad, who come to camp because they love the whole camp experience. Then there are those, like me, who grudgingly participate because they are getting paid.

Whatever the case, camp counselors do little actual counseling. Most of the time, I was merely herding kids from one activity to another and trying to get them to complete their Bible lesson sheets.

With the youngest campers, I was trying to get them excited (but not too excited!) about beating an opposing team in water balloon fighting.

With the older campers, I was mostly counting noses to ensure that everyone made it back from campfire time. Again: very little counseling.

As the only adult in my cabin, I'd gather the boys each night at lights out and give them a stern warning: "I'll be outside patrolling the grounds. You'd better stay in here and go to sleep, or there will be serious consequences."

Serious consequences are what you threaten people with when you have no real idea what might happen. It's not nearly as threatening as the truth: "I'm going to be in the woods, kissing your other counselor, and I don't wish to be bothered."

That week flew by. My co-counselor was named Lana. She sang for worship services during the week, and I thought I heard angels. I saw her looking at me while I led devotions. I would have led those devotions right into the deep end of the pool if she'd kept smiling at me. She was perfect. And then...

She got back into the van. The other worship leaders, her fellow students from a college that's about half of America away, were friends with a guy who still thought he might be her boyfriend. The unavoidable dust cloud rose as the van pulls away.

Lana was waving. I was waving, and even the almost 100 percent uncounseled campers in our soon-to-dissolve family could tell something important had happened.

# 27

# People Used to Write Letters

Two days after that historic week of camp ended, I was back to my summer-and-weekends youth minster gig. The senior minister asked me how the week went. (I should note that he was "senior" in title only. He was maybe 30.)

I was 22, and the answer to all of my most fervent prayers was 19—and 600 miles away.

I told the senior minister that Lana was perfect. "She's the exact kind of person I want to marry."

"Why don't you marry her, then?" he replied. So easy to say, but I could not figure out how it could possibly work. I was a senior in college for the second time around. She was a sophomore who wanted to be an overseas missionary doctor. It was simply not feasible. And believe me, I tried to *feas* it.

Then I got a letter from her. Her music group was going to work one more weekend at a camp about an hour from my weekend job. Could I maybe meet her?

*Yes, I am definitely supposed to be there!* I thought.

That weekend I told Lana I'd always wanted to name my firstborn son after my paternal grandfather, Riley. She agreed it was a cool name. That pretty much settled it. She went back to her school. I went back to mine. And we wrote letters.

Lots of letters. Every day. Every single day. We shared every thought and feeling we could put into words. This made us closer than 100 pizza-and-movie dates ever could. She transferred to my school at the semester. As I had only half a year to go, it made sense. Plus, I'd given up on soccer, so sports would not get in our way.

Then I met Lana's family. They were unimpressed. That first encounter went like this:

Her aunts, grandmother, and mother gathered in the family room. I remember it as a sea of beehive hairdos and floral print dresses and general awkwardness. They examined this male specimen who came from a big city and a small nondenomination.

Even though these relatives were part of an actual denomination, I thought things were going okay—until Lana's father arrived. A tractor mechanic, he entered through the garage, grimy from work. Meanwhile, I was a college student who had just arrived from doing…not much, on that day or ever.

I rose from the sea of hairdos and floral prints to shake his hand. He looked me up and down before announcing, "He's too big to whip." With that, he headed for, and I am not kidding about this, his gun room. The room where he loaded shells for his shotgun. We didn't speak again for almost a year.

Then Lana met my family. Immediately (and predictably), they preferred her to me. For the rest of the courtship, my family gave off a distinct *Don't screw this up, Dan* vibe. They did this by dropping subtle hints, such as, "Dan, don't screw this up."

That semester at college was anything but magical. Girls who would not give me the time of day were still less than pleased to know that the eligible guy count on campus had been diminished by one.

Meanwhile, Lana and I did not invest time in any relationship save our own. We were like monks who devoted all their time kissing until they had to retreat to their separate dorms. Perhaps we weren't that much like monks. But my point is that we didn't socialize outside of our bubble. We just kissed and planned for the future.

And that future would kick off with a wedding.

# 28

# The Wedding Singer

Do you know the word *venue*? It's a French word that means "place." But it also means, "You are paying way more for this wedding than you should be."

Lana's and my wedding wasn't in a venue. It was in a church, like all the other important things in life: weddings, funerals, Eagle Scout recognition ceremonies (not that I ever got that far), and men's prayer breakfasts. These were things that happened in churches.

You would have the ceremony in the sanctuary, followed by a reception in the fellowship hall—later referred to by the trendier, more corporate-sounding, multipurpose room. (Multipurpose room is overstating things, by the way. You're going to hold potluck dinners in that room. You'll also do wedding receptions and, perhaps, junior church. "Three-purpose room" would be much more accurate.)

I'd recently turned 23. My bride was just about to turn 20. If you're good at math, you have determined that we got married less than a year after we met. Would I recommend this? Probably not. If my own kids had wanted to do something similar, I would not have been as cool about it as my parents were. Even my in-laws were okay with it. Such was the undeniable power of our love or something.

When I say we had no money at the time, it's not a figure of speech. The amount of money we had was none. Our 401 was not O(K). Lana's wedding dress was probably the biggest expense we incurred, and it's no exaggeration to say that now I spend that same amount of money on two pairs of shoes and an ironic T-shirt.

The ceremony itself was also very typical of the time. Our church's not-so-senior minister shared the duties with my dad. It was all standard stuff, with one exception.

Our friends provided the exception.

As noted, I was young. I chose friends not by loyalty or fealty or any of the other-*tys*. I chose friends by how much they made me laugh. My ushers, in particular, have gone on to accomplish great things. They are what you'd call good Kingdom men. But at the time of the wedding, they were just very funny guys.

They laughed hard and often, and that became very important on this, our most special of days. My wife, as I've mentioned, is a lovely singer, and as lovely singers in her town used to do, she took voice lessons from a very formidable woman.

This formidable woman sang "The Lord's Prayer" at our wedding. Did you know there's a song version of this famous prayer? Oh, there is; there really is. It's a very serious, opera-style song. Opera-style is what nonsingers call anything that sounds remotely fancy, and this was super fancy. It had tremolo (that intentional shaky-voice thing), and it went on and on. From where I was standing (near the front, as it was my wedding), only I could see my ushers at the back of the church. The song struck them as funny. They started laughing.

They giggled. They chuckled. They chortled. Finally, they guffawed and bent over laughing, secure in the knowledge that, with only me and my intended looking in their direction, no one could see them.

But I could see them, and, being human, I started laughing too. Then my bride started laughing. I'm told that from the pews it appeared as if we were overcome with emotion, trying to get a grip on the poignant proceedings. The reality? We had started laughing, and we couldn't stop. We laughed through the whole ceremony. Laughing at embarrassing moments doesn't make them go away, and you can be pretty sure that not everyone, everywhere, is going to laugh with you. But laughing does something for the heart, and for the soul, that nothing else can do.

Thirtysome years later, Lana and I still laugh a lot. Usually when we're supposed to, and pretty much in any and all venues.

# 29

# Tom Sawyer's Car Wash

When you don't have a denominational structure in your church's tradition, getting a job as a newly graduated senior can be tricky. This was the first time I was looking for a job where my dad didn't just "know a guy."

So I graduated, I got married, and then I went to my home church to get ordained. Technically, this means that a recognized church (recognized by *whom*, you might wonder) sets you aside as a dedicated practitioner of…not much. And nobody really noticed that I had been set aside. I was just sitting there, set aside.

However, I needed a job, so I went back to drywall taping.

Here's the way a construction job like drywall taping works: You work when there's work. Unfortunately, there is no work a lot of the time. Construction is a strike-while-the-iron-is-hot and make-hay-while-the-sun-shines deal—to borrow expressions from two other kinds of jobs.

Drywall taping wasn't a bad job. You go to work as the sun is coming up, because there is often no electricity at the sites yet. You quit when the sun goes down because, again, it's hard to see the seams in the dark.

We'd clean our tools by the light of the truck headlights. Then I'd head home, exhausted. But Lana and I were young and in love, and the time passed quickly, if you know what I'm not saying. Then it was back to work at dawn.

It was not a bad life, but not the life I wanted. Meanwhile, my alma mater was sending out résumés to churches that looked to the school for exciting new faces in the fast-paced and challenging world of youth ministry. Or something like that. And that's how a couple of churches found me.

The first church that interviewed me was in Hannibal, Missouri. If that sounds familiar to you, it's probably because of Mark Twain. That's right, America's beloved humorist, the creator of Tom Sawyer and Huck Finn, grew up in Hannibal. He set his heroes' adventures in that town and the river that ran through it.

I'm going to discuss Hannibal only as I remember it more than three decades ago. And I'm not going to provide you enough details to visit the city and fact-check me. But, man, that place was like no place I've seen before or since. Everything (*every single thing*) bore some kind of Mark Twain tie-in. Hannibal looked like a Mark Twain movie set.

Becky Thatcher's Dry Cleaners sat across the street from Becky Thatcher's Diner. Huck Finn's Optometry was just up the street. Every third building had Tom Sawyer worked into its name. For a guy who tried so hard to avoid work, there were an awful lot of businesses bearing his likeness.

The people I interviewed with at the church gave me the impression they were not impressed with me. I thought I might have to build my own raft to float out of there. They never called me back. This was probably best for everyone involved.

So it was back to drywall taping—mixing buckets of drywall mud, hauling those buckets everywhere, cleaning the buckets, and starting over the next day. Still not drinking beer with the guys after work and still wondering what was going to happen next.

Meanwhile, my mediocre résumé continued to make the rounds.

# 30

# A Brand-New Mexico

If you didn't grow up in New Mexico, you probably know as much about it as you do about Hannibal, Missouri. When I got a call from a New Mexican church, I had no idea how long that long-distance call had traveled. New Mexico, I learned later, has seven distinct "life zones," which support various kinds of plants, animals, flora, and fauna. Some of them are beautiful. There are desert landscapes that look like paintings and mountains that look like other paintings. There are thriving cities and scenic spots that are home to flourishing artistic communities.

And there was the place we settled. It's none of the good things I just mentioned. In fact, the only thing I can tell you for sure is that it's a really great place to fail as a youth minister.

There were no early signs I'd be a good youth minister, and I didn't grow into the job either. Remember when I explained that I'm more of a "Dan" than a "Danny"? Youth ministry is a Danny job. Or maybe a Daniel, because there are two ways you can win in the job.

| Danny | Daniel |
| --- | --- |
| Super fun guy | Very smart, studious guy |
| Knows how to swim | Knows Greek |
| Knows how to skate | Knows Hebrew |
| Pretty good at all sports | Working on a doctorate |
| Kids love him | Kids are impressed by him |
| Parents love him | Parents respect him |
| Gets offers from bigger churches | Gets offers to teach in seminaries |

| Dan | |
| --- | --- |
| None of the above | |

The people at the church in New Mexico could not have been nicer to Lana and me. They welcomed us with open arms. Plus, the job came with a parsonage. Parsonage is a churchy word for "house," and it was a nice little rancher on a quiet street. The street was quiet because it was full of retirees. Sounds nice, right? Here's the thing: Retirees have lots of free time, and they use that free time to work on their lawns. The lawns in our neighborhood were perfect. There's a certain kind of grass that grows lush and green even in the not-pretty part of the desert. All you have to do is go out each day and encourage each individual blade. Our yard, by contrast, was mostly dust.

And that dusty theme carried to the inside of the house. In the desert, you can't keep the dust off of anything. You have to blink frequently or your eyes will dry out. Look it up. It's true. Okay, don't look it up. That's actually not true, but I'm not exaggerating much. You had to dust every day. And this futile effort was an apt metaphor for how I felt about my job, which seemed impossible and heartbreaking.

Turns out, youth ministry is at least partly marketing. You have to believe in the programs you're planning. Sometimes you have to actually believe a kid would be better off at your church than the one down the street. I never figured out how to do that.

Cable TV was just starting to take hold, and I had no answer to that. Kids wanted their MTV. To be honest, so did I.

Also, college did not prepare me for the office hours I had to put in each week. (Or maybe it did, but I didn't pay attention.) Other guys who went to school with me turned out to be great youth ministers. And senior ministers too.

About a month into the job, I started talking to my wife about leaving. Not just New Mexico, but youth ministry altogether. She had just started nursing school, and wow, did I mess that plan up.

First, she left her great school to join me for a semester at mine. By this time, she had decided to be a nurse, and there were no nursing classes at Bible college. There was a surprisingly good junior college in New Mexico, so she had started taking some classes there. When I started to make noises about leaving, she asked if we could stay put until she finished the two-year program. And it looked like that might happen, but first I had to learn how to drive a bus.

Why? So that I could take kids to camp. That's why.

# 31

# Does This Bus Stop at the Top of the Mountain?

As part of my new job, I had to/got to work several weeks of camp. The church was in the not-pretty part of the desert, with nothing but flat vistas as far as the eye could see. But the camp? Oh, the camp was in the mountains.

And the best way to get a bunch of kids into the mountains, apparently, was in a full-size school bus. A youth pastor named Danny could drive a bus because he'd been riding motorcycles and jet skis since birth. And a youth pastor named Daniel could learn bus-driving by tapping the power of his keen mind.

Meanwhile, this youth pastor named Dan was pretty sure he was going to die at the bottom of a mountain.

Practicing the bus driving wasn't so bad. The good thing about the desert is that there's plenty of room to turn a full-sized school bus around. I got the hang of it eventually, getting high-centered only once.

In case you are wondering, here's how to high-center a bus: You drive it across something, like a busy street, crossways. Your front wheels do just fine, but the middle part of the bus gets stuck on a median. Your back wheels aren't on the ground firmly enough to push the bus forward, and the front wheels are also not on solid ground anymore. The massive bus is suspended by its low-hanging midsection. Only a bulldozer can pull it off the road.

Was the bulldozer driver laughing while he helped me? Of course he was. You know that cowboy-laughing-at-a-city-slicker laugh? I heard that a lot in New Mexico. To be fair, if the boot were on the other foot, I'd have laughed too. In fact, when I look back on it now...I still cannot laugh. Maybe if I live to be really, really old, I'll think it's funny. But not yet. I kind of laugh. It's not a super hardy laugh, it's more of a chuckle, but hey, a laugh's a laugh, right?

Eventually I earned my Class C driver's license. I was a legal (hopefully not lethal) bus driver. But driving a bus all over the not-pretty desert is one thing. Driving it into the mountains is another.

The mountain road to camp rose at an angle so steep the massive bus engine could barely handle it. I'm not exaggerating when I say that you could look out the side windows and not see the road, just the desert floor getting farther and farther away as the bus lumbered almost straight upward.

But what you *could* see were the rusted chassis of cars that had not made it up the hill. A graveyard of failed attempts served as a silent reminder of what could happen. This was not lost on me, and the last thing I needed as I attempted to assay this mountain was a busload of screaming middle schoolers.

So I scared them. I told them that any distraction—a loud voice, a hearty laugh, a sudden movement, or breathing too much—would result in their certain death. I said this to them in a voice they'd never heard from me before, wearing an expression they had never seen before.

Did I scar them as well as scare them? Possibly. But it worked. They were quiet, and we made it to camp. Then they had a week to get over the trauma before it was time to roll home.

The campground was pretty in its way. It was located in the mountains, and if you like mountains, you would probably like it, I guess. It was mostly rocks and dirt. I don't remember much about it because I knew I had to ride the brakes through the valley of the shadow of death at the end of the week. And talking to the other youth ministers at length after lights-out made me sure that my wife was not going to get to finish that second year of nursing school—because my time as a youth minister was just about done.

# 32

# Church, Junior

Lest you think I didn't give youth ministry the old college try, here's a typical Sunday for me. (But keep in mind that I quit college once, so "college try" is for me, perhaps, not that big of a deal.)

My main responsibilities as a youth minister were youth group (high schoolers) and junior church (first through sixth graders). I had taught high schoolers at camp and on weekends, so that was pretty easy. But junior church was a whole 'nother deal, as they say.

The kids were corralled in the multipurpose room, junior church being one of the three purposes that constituted "multi." Here, they mumbled/sang a few choruses. This wasn't camp, where volume was encouraged over worship experience. This was *church*, so a level of serious devotion was implied and then immediately ignored as the kids shouted/sang about marching and flying and shooting guns. The militaristic nature of the song these eight-year-olds were rocking was never noticed, much less mentioned. They slaughtered the Lord's enemies and then sat still, waiting for the sermon.

Or tried to. A big day in junior church was maybe 30 kids. And 30 kids don't do anything quietly. So, in the tradition of youth workers everywhere, I made a game out of the sermon. Here's how it worked:

> Today, we're going to talk about Jonah. God had a special
> job for Jonah, but Jonah didn't want to do that job. God
> wanted Jonah to go to Nineveh, but Jonah got on a boat
> and went the other way…

You know the rest of the story. But the kids didn't, so they sat there listening closely and making mental notes of the details. Because that's how they would be able to win the game I made up.

After the sermon, I'd split the room into two groups, left side vs. right side, or the more popular boys vs. girls, and the game was afoot. I'd ask questions. Each of these questions was worth—brace yourself—1,000 points!

How is this even possible? How can an eight- or nine-year-old amass 1,000 points with a single answer? It's crazy! No one has ever imagined this many points! Madness! Or, you know, totally made up. But it pretty much worked. When the kids were especially squirrel-like, the point value was set at…are you ready? One million points per question! What would you *not* do for such a bounty of points? Truly, Christmas had come early to this corner of New Mexico.

But sometimes Christmas got held up a little. Junior church ended with cookies and juice. This was not biblical, per se, but it was foundational to these young churchgoers. They looked forward to the cookies and juice with a level of anticipation that approached epiphany. So it really hurt the deal when one of the volunteers forgot his part and didn't bring either the juice or the cookies.

Wisely, these two responsibilities were split between separate volunteer families, and fortunately, we were never let down on both sides. But every now and then, the juice parent or the cookie parent would mess up. It happens. I made lemonade out of this lack of lemons.

At the start of the sermon (point value raised to one million since we were short a snack item), I'd feign disappointment at the attention level of the assembled youngsters. This was easy, as they were rarely paying attention unless a bribe was involved. With a somber expression usually reserved for bus-manners speeches, I'd tell them that their poor behavior had already cost them juice. Would they like to try for cookies? Because they could lose them too.

Sobered by the loss of juice, they clammed up. Or vice versa, depending on which snack had been forgotten. It worked like a charm, and I hardly felt bad about the omission-style partial truth.

The kids who appreciated the juice and/or cookies the most were the "bus kids." Every Sunday a volunteer (sometimes, by default, me) took a van—not the full-sized school bus, but a full-sized van—and drove into a rougher, poorer part of the already pretty rough and pretty poor town.

There, on the corners of streets that were not exactly streets and between houses that were not exactly houses (more like campers and other kind of makeshift quarters), we'd pick up a half dozen kids or so.

These kids came from homes where English was not the main language, and maybe not even spoken at all, but their English was fine. When they saw it was me at the wheel, they were disappointed, because the Donut Lady, as her name suggests, always had boxes of donuts riding shotgun, and everyone got a couple of donuts before they got to church.

So I was usually greeted with, "Where's the Donut Lady, Don?" Their English was solid, but they couldn't make the nasal *a* sound that formed the middle of my name. I'd explain they were stuck with me, and they'd usually take this loss in stride. There was at least juice, or a cookie, maybe both, awaiting them at church.

I'd love to tell you that the bus kids were embraced by everyone in the church at large and lives were changed. That didn't happen. The volunteers who got to know them loved them. That was a very easy thing to do. But not all the parents took to them, and some of the adults were downright *anti*. And to be fair, the kids were mostly there for the snacks and maybe the points.

I still miss those kids, and several of the high schoolers even, kind of, pretty much. However, I don't miss the job. And once I talked it through with my surprisingly patient and wise senior minister, it became clear that it was time to move on.

But to what?

# 33

# Lobo

Youth ministers work nights and weekends, and often my wife could come with me for youth group outings to fun places like roller rinks or swimming pools. But there were many other times when she was home alone. Because of this, some friends gifted her a dog.

I know! I was as surprised as you are. Apparently, these friends were at the Laundromat, and they heard whimpering. This isn't uncommon in Laundromats, but there was also the sound of some kind of struggle, which drew them to a corner of the room. That's where they found a puppy in a box.

They fell in love with the little guy immediately, and, as they already had their own lovable bundles of fur, they thought of us. I say "lovable bundle of fur" because I think that's how pet people talk. I was not, and am not, and do not foresee becoming a pet person.

Pets provide endless hours, nay, years of unconditional love and companionship. No home is complete without one. These are the kind of statements I have never uttered. But the dog was so cute that my wife was enamored. As for me, I couldn't see the downside, so we had ourselves a dog. Turns out there was a downside.

Laundromats are rough on dogs, apparently. This one, whom we named Lobo because it sounded tough and New Mexican, was crazy. He had several doggie diseases, the most pronounced of which was rickets. What rickets does to a dog, on the off chance that you don't know, is a bowing of all four legs. Lobo looked like a fur-covered pair of parentheses. He couldn't walk a straight line. If he tried to go from north go south, he'd end up southeast. This was a dog headed for Florida but bound to hit Houston. He walked like a drunken sailor, and his fur always looked a little bedraggled and wet, even when it was not draggled and perfectly dry.

Lobo could run, though! He could run like the wind—if the wind happened to be crazy. He ran exclusively in circles, exclusively in our family room. Around and around and around, following whatever inner drive drove him.

When we knew we were going to move, Lobo could not come with us. The desert was his home, we told ourselves. He wouldn't be happy anywhere else. He found a good home and has since, I'm sure, gone on to whatever canine heaven dogs go to. Perhaps there he can walk a straight line if he wants to. But I'll bet he chooses to run in circles.

# 34

# Card Tricks

At this point, my young wife and I formed a plan: Move back into my parents' house (again!) and live there while I went to…some other kind of college? Maybe to be an English teacher, while nursing school for her moved to yet another, further-back back burner?

Okay, it wasn't much of a plan.

Again, my parents were surprisingly cool with the idea of my leaving the job I'd been ordained to do and living with my wife in their basement. But things didn't unfold that way.

One day, I was sitting in my luxuriously appointed youth minister office reading *Rolling Stone* magazine. Why did I have such a nice office? That was part of the problem. The guy I replaced at my youth ministry job was a guy I could never truly replace. He left that job and went to teach youth ministry at a theological seminary. That's how good he was at youth ministry. And to acknowledge that, he'd been given a fabulous office in a freshly renovated building. It had wood paneling, back when wood paneling was a good thing. A massive oak desk, which is still a good thing. A chair that supported lumbar vertebrae I did not know I had. Terrific.

I had no idea what do to in there, so I was reading that magazine front to back.

In the back was an ad that said, "Do you think you could write ten funny greeting cards?" For reasons that will be Question Number 1 when I get to heaven, I thought, *Sure, why not?* And I sent ten greeting card ideas to an address in Kansas City.

And then nothing happened. The youth ministry job means you are not home in the daytime or the evening or the weekend. Answering machines were fancy things only rich people had. I was not rich or fancy.

But long after I'd forgotten sending those ideas to that address, I got a call and was actually in the room when the phone rang.

The man on the phone said he liked my ideas. Could I maybe try ten more? he wondered. Again, with a confidence that came from having no clue what was at stake, I said, "Sure."

. . . . . . . . . . . .

Our farewell party was, for us, a tearless affair. If you know anything about youth ministry, you know that's not good. If Frankenstein's monster were a youth minister, if Dracula were a "nights only" youth minister, some middle school girl would cry when he left. Nobody cried when I left. That's how bad I was at youth ministry.

Immediately after the tearless party, I drove to the nearest airport, three hours away. I flew to Kansas City.

I grew up outside Chicago. I knew that if you went east, there was New York. If you went west, there was Los Angeles. What else was there? Didn't know, didn't care. Such was the big-city arrogance of a kid who lived in the suburbs.

It turned out that Kansas City was a place with an airport and everything. I had two days of interviews. When that was complete, I called my wife of almost two years and asked, "What if we don't move back home to Chicago but instead move to Kansas City? Because I have a job there now."

Fortunately, she agreed and we changed our destination to the middle of the country. We had a small car packed to the roof and a midsized U-Haul, ready for on a road trip across America. What could go wrong?

Turns out, quite a bit.

# 35

# Fight or Flight

Three months into my new job, I met a guy who was also a new hire and had come to Kansas City from a similar distance. Because he was some kind of genius, he got the big company to pay for his move, including packers and movers and fancy stuff like that.

Not the Taylors. We packed our own truck, and, proud possessor of a Class C license, I drove it from New Mexico to Kansas City. What a bad idea.

We relocated in the middle of the winter, which doesn't matter in New Mexico, but it's a much bigger deal in the middle of the country. We drove straight into a blizzard, and I was basically at the helm of a giant sail. The wind caught it and whipped it into oncoming traffic. Then the crosswind tried to take it straight into a surprisingly deep ditch.

Meanwhile, my wife in the car ahead was having, as I imagined, the time of her life, driving along, singing a song, and every now and then looking for me in the rearview mirror. Chances are, you've never had to follow my wife anywhere. Count your stars. They are lucky. She cares deeply and passionately about many things, but the person following her will never be one of those things. And remember, this was BC (before cell phones).

Moreover, here is a thing I haven't mentioned before: I have no sense of direction. None. Genetic defect? Nature? Nurture? No telling, but I don't know east from west from a hole in the ground. I was staring at that vanishing license plate as the snow blew and the truck tried to slide sideways, and her car just…disappeared. Then the cops came. All the cops.

A charming thing about small towns is the cooperation that they embody. Everyone pitches in and helps harvest the crop or deliver the calf or whatever they need to do. One of those things is that, every now and then, they decide to test the response times of their emergency vehi-cles. Ever heard of this? Here's how it works: Every police car and every firetruck and every ambulance blow through town on an appointed day to see how long it takes for all of them to respond to whatever might befall them.

The locals know about this, and passersby...well, they get waved off the road and have to just chill in a parking lot while every single emer-gency vehicle speeds down the street.

So I was sitting in the hardware store parking lot while every vehicle with a siren sped past. Meanwhile, Lana had lost sight of me. She was, one presumes, mildly curious as to my whereabouts, but she was still speeding along at her preferred 80 or 90 mph. Then she saw a cop car with the lights on behind her. *My time has come,* she thought, but the car passed her. Then another police vehicle, then a firetruck, then an ambu-lance, and still no sign of her husband. This was disturbing. She pulled over and wondered how she would go about meeting new people.

Eventually, the roads reopened, and I was waved back onto the high-way. I trudged along, and in a few minutes, I spied our car on the shoul-der. Did I handle this well? Did I say, "These things happen" and chuckle in an endearing manner?

No. Lana and I had, to date, the biggest fight of our married life, but most of the shouting was lost in the whipping wind and the falling snow. I implored her to drive slower. She encouraged me to drive faster, and eventually, somehow, we got to the outskirts of Kansas City.

And then things really got interesting.

# 36

# A Mice Little Apartment

The greeting card company where I got my first post–youth minister job is called Hallmark Cards. Maybe you've heard of them. Hallmark card shops are located all over the place, but the main office is in Kansas City. Hallmark offers a relocation service that helps new hires find a place to live. However, my new boss thought it would be a good idea to skip using this service in favor of one of his own employees. The thinking was that the employee was a young guy. Thus, Young Employee Guy would be able to show me where all the hip, happening people lived.

This would have been a good idea if my wife and I had been either hip or happening. My coworker-to-be showed us trendy little places in a part of town that was full of bars and restaurants and cool nightlife-style things. We were not into that, as indicated by the fact that I just called them "cool nightlife-style things." I don't think that's what the actual cool nightlife denizens call them. We just wanted whatever was cheap.

So we grabbed one of those free papers that businesses used to have stacked up in the doorways of diners. We looked for the cheapest place we could find. It's easy to shop when your only qualifier is, "What's cheapest?"

We took the cheapest place, unloaded our boxes from the rental truck, and headed home to visit family for a few days before the job started. That visit was nice. The apartment we returned to was less so.

Walking in, you could tell something bad had happened. Not through any kind of psychic means. Just by smell. And using that same now-offended sense, you could even pinpoint the location of the bad thing.

Remember when refrigerators used to have coils in the back? I don't know the mechanics of it, but somehow that's what kept your frozen pizza *frozen*: a series of thin metal tubes on the back of the fridge.

These coils also attracted mice, apparently. Not healthy mice, or at least this one wasn't. This was a mouse who had lost the will to live and had decided that weaving himself into the refrigerator coils would be a fitting final resting place.

As far as we knew, he'd been there the entire time we were gone. It sure smelled that way. And there was no way I was going to deal with him. Say what you will about the suburbs; they are not full of dead mice. This was a job for the country girl. My wife pried the carcass out of the coils and into a bag. I was in charge of taking him to the Dumpster. (Or her. I do not know how to identify mouse genders. I can pretty much get "dead" and "alive." That's about it for categories.) I took the dead guy or gal to the Dumpster at the corner of the parking lot.

The blizzard we'd been traveling/fighting in had not melted yet, and more snow had snowed on top of it, so there were several feet to slog through to get around outside.

I was on my way back from the Dumpster. It was about ten o'clock at night and snowing again, and I met a guy in the parking lot. He asked me if I could give him a ride to an ATM. For reasons I will never fully understand, I said, "Sure!" Away we went, slipping and sliding in my little car, while my wife began to wonder what was so complicated about dumping a mouse in a Dumpster. I took the guy to an ATM, where he got some cash. Then he wanted me to take him to a bar. Again, I said, "Sure!"

I dropped him at a bar and headed home.

I had no real idea where home was. We had lived there for a matter of hours. And I should remind you at this point that I am directionally challenged, as they say. It was now about eleven o'clock. The snow continued to fall.

Much, much later, I found the apartment, along with a wife who was the kind of angry that's made angrier by worry but also alleviated somewhat by relief. It's a powerful cocktail of emotions. We went to bed fretful.

It was about four o'clock in the morning when the guy from the parking lot began banging on our apartment door. Except it wasn't our apartment. There was a landing where four different doors led to the four apartments on that floor, but one of the ways this place was cheap was that if you knocked hard enough on a door, or not even very hard at all, each door shook like everyone had company calling.

I grabbed my baseball bat, which was the only thing we'd unpacked. I peeked out the peephole and saw that he was across the hall. Feeling like I'd said everything to him that I wanted to say on our car trip, I went back to bed, only to discover that it was possible to sleep even more fretfully than I already had. You can be fretful and still add more fret, so you're not really *full* of fret. We started looking for a new place to live the next day.

The place we found was great! And way too expensive for us! In fact, it was brand new, and they were offering a deal where you signed up for a six-month lease and one month was free. We lived there six months and then moved to a more reasonable location.

The mouse house kept our deposit since we were technically breaking a lease with the property manager. Seemed fair. The not-surprisingly-bitter rental agent in the office said, "It seems like you wanted to live here only until you could find somewhere better."

I replied, "I hope everyone is doing that!"

Sometimes we drive within a few miles of the place for this or that reason, and every time we feel a small chill. And most of that chill is directed at me for making my bride pry a dead mouse out of the fridge.

# 37

# Only When the Doors Are Open

Not bragging, which is what people always say right before bragging, but my wife and I, especially BC (before children) were pretty hot commodities as far as church members went. If you had a church that was a part of our nondenomination, most likely we'd come the first Sunday available once we had moved to your town. After that, you couldn't get rid of us.

And we were not mere Sunday morning attendees. We're talking Sunday nights and Wednesday nights too. Throw in tithing, which we did without really even thinking about it, and, well, as I said: It's hard not to brag.

But wait, there's more! One of us can play the piano and sing. The other can teach Sunday school for any and all ages. And together, we served as youth group sponsors. We were a church dream team, mostly because there's usually not a lot of competition for this particular team.

It can be weird when a guy with a preaching degree comes to your church—but not as the preacher. Some pastors don't like it at all. There can be that assumed, "I'd have done it another way" thing between you and the official pastor. Conversations can be awkward.

However, when the new nonstaff preacher was merely a *youth minister*, well, that's like having a neighbor with a truck. Your new sofa bed delivery worries are over! (So to speak.)

No one thinks they can do what senior pastors do: the hospital visits, the weddings, the funerals, the weekly sermons (in our tradition, two per Sunday) and the endless administrative whatnot. It's clear that being a senior pastor is a tough job.

But what do youth ministers do? You fill some water balloons, you organize a trip to the nearest amusement park, and you come up with something to do for all the kids who aren't going to prom. When fall comes around, you think of something for the kids who aren't trick-or-treating. How hard can it be?

If you have a sucker...I mean, willing volunteer couple, it's like Christmas. We youth-group-led. Lana played piano. I taught a Sunday school class and passed out Communion and collected offering. It sounds like a lot of work when it's all grouped together like that, but it was a good time.

In fact, not having to be a staff member made everything seem easy and fun by comparison. Here's a secret I learned early on: No one criticizes a volunteer. Everyone has some "constructive criticism" to offer the paid guy, but the volunteer? Not a word. And we really did enjoy it. We made friends, no one drowned when we took kids to the local water park, and the Sunday school class had more people the second year than it had the first.

We could have stayed there forever, but a church had been planted just a few miles down the road. Before long, those people came looking for us.

# Rental Church

The phenomenon of new churches renting schools for Sunday services was just beginning, and our established church hosted a phone marathon to get the brand-new church off the ground—and into a local middle school. There was a simple and proven plan in place, but I discovered that I could get onboard with only part of this plan.

Back when everyone had a landline phone, you could get a list of all the phone numbers in a given geographic zone. How? No idea. I'm not sure you could do it now, and there wouldn't be that many landlines anyway, but you used to be able to pinpoint a town, or, in the case of our tightly packed suburban area, a certain number of square miles that seemed like a reasonable distance from your church or school's location.

Then, armed with a dauntingly large number of numbers, volunteers gather for several evenings and call the homes in the designated area.

I couldn't do it. Cold calls were the part of youth ministry I dreaded the most. The elders and the staff had to do it at the New Mexico church. Meanwhile, the youngest elder and I would take a stack of prospects and leave the church office. Then we would drive slowly by the homes and determine that it looked like nobody was home. Or they were home but eating dinner. Or there was a mean dog.

The upshot? We'd go drink coffee and come back to the office, reporting that we struck out.

So there was no way I was going to do this kind of recruiting when I wasn't even on the payroll. I ended up taking pizza orders for the callers, going to get the pizzas, delivering the pizzas to the callers, and grabbing napkins from the multipurpose room, stuff like that.

The callers did a bang-up job without me, probably energized by the promptly delivered and cheerfully served pizza. On our first Sunday in a school building, 200 people showed up. My wife and I helped with that first service, then went back to our "old" church.

About two years into the rental experiment, everything was going well. However, the new church needed another singer/pianist and another teacher. They asked us nicely, and we parted on friendly terms with our more traditional, in-a-building church. We headed for the new, in-a-school church.

When your church meets in a school, you have to set the whole thing up. When I was a kid and we did this, it was easy. The congregations were small, and the tech was low. There was no sound system—the piano was already there. Basically, church was just Bibles, hymnals, and Communion stuff. Not so at the church-in-a-school. There were speakers and instruments and microphones and endless miles of cords and video equipment—including one very specific and impossible-to-deal-with element.

We had to supply our own projection screen and our own frame and stand for the screen. The frame was made out of lightweight metal and was, perhaps, 12 feet across and 10 feet high. The screen itself was more like 10 feet across and 8 feet high. See the problem? A team of 40 to 50 volunteers each grabbed a handful of screen and pulled for all their worth. Then industrial snaps were snapped into place and hammered down with sledgehammers, and, voilà, the screen was secured. You tested it by bouncing an eight-month-old elephant on it. This is only a slight exaggeration. The elephant could be as young as six months.

The heartbreakingly difficult to deploy screen went up on the stage. The stage was composed of four equal sections that were like tables with eight-inch legs. The stage was going to hold several people, speakers, and musical instruments, so it had to be very strong. This meant that each of the four matching sections was very heavy. Go outside and try to lift your car. If you can, the stage would have been easy for you. Otherwise, it was a killer.

Setup was done by rotating crews. Every couple of weeks, you'd get to the school a few hours ahead and stay an hour or more after. The rotation was every third week or so, and I'd become accustomed to not working every single Sunday.

I came up with a plan where I still had to work every Sunday, but only a little bit. Calling my own shot, if you will.

This plan went about as well as most of my other plans.

# 39

# Reading the Signs

As noted in the previous chapter, the phone-a-thon brought 200 people to our new church that first week. After that, attendance settled, as research showed it would, at about 100.

From there, the church grew steadily. People who lived nearby came to check us out, and others were invited by friends. In fact, the model worked so well that several other schools began hosting start-up churches.

When your church is meeting in a school, how can your people find the *right* school? Remember, this was an era when there was no map on the phone in your pocket. That's because there *was* no phone in your pocket. Your phone was back at home, wired to a wall.

The good news is that the landline was how your church found you in the first place. The bad news is that the suburban neighborhoods all looked about the same. And the schools all looked *exactly* the same.

To find the church you sought, you needed a sign. I volunteered myself to put out the signs full-time, every Sunday. I know this sounds like a lot of work, but we were already going to church anyway, and the sign tasks let me escape setting up that semipermanent stage every couple of weeks. Worth it.

We got four signs professionally made out of the same plastic polyfibers that form the space shuttle. Probably. They were sturdy. They looked great and were slightly larger than the average real estate lawn sign.

Directions and service times for our church were clearly printed. The signs' sides were made of angle iron that came to points. It came to points because, if signs are not sharp enough, there's no way they can really tear up your car when you transport them. I don't know if you've ever tried to tear up a car, but if you want to, an angle iron sign is certainly one of your most effective implements. The steel is stronger than anything it's going to hit, and the point is good for really cutting into not just the headliner of your hatchback but also the floorboards. It's simply a matter of where you place the signs, and/or how much they bounce around in transit.

For this reason, and for some others that are less important, I bought a small truck. It was pretty cool, and I loved it. That made it hard to throw the signs in it, but if you have a truck, you're supposed to tear it up. So I let the signs rip.

When you do this every Sunday, year-round, there are going to be times when it's you and your signs against the frozen tundra. To alleviate this natural phenomenon, I brought a gallon of hot water in a jug and poured it on the ground before hammering in my signs. This worked pretty well most of the time. For those other times, I carried a sledge-hammer and a shovel. I was not playing around.

I took my sign-planting role so seriously that I didn't pay a lot of attention to other drivers. When you're operating a motor vehicle, that's a bad thing.

One of the church signs had to be placed in the middle of a median. To place the sign there, I'd park in the left turn lane with my hazard lights on. I was parked there early one Sunday morning, with no traffic in sight. My lights blinked while I plunged the sign into the ground. A car came up behind me just as I hopped back into the truck and took off.

It's a funny expression: "hazard lights." He (or she; I never found out) saw the hazard lights, and a hazard ensued. The first driver had tried to maneuver around me and collided with yet another driver.

My sign delivery route took me around the block and then back by the scene of the accident. That's how I got to see *yet another car* join in the mayhem. Now there was a three-car pileup that was kind of my fault, but not really.

What is the protocol in a situation like this? I am unsure to this day, but, as I rolled past the scene, I realized I was witnessing three parties who were never going to attend our church-in-a-school.

# 40

# Firefighters Work Sundays

Were lives changed at the various iterations of church that met in various schools? Of course they were. Stirring music stirred, and riveting sermons riveted. Communion was communed. But it's the accidents I tend to remember because it's pretty easy to have church. The hard part is packing and unpacking our church-in-a-school every single Sunday, 52 Sundays a year. The challenges we faced and overcame still stand out.

For example, a really handy guy in our congregation made us some really handy boxes that were the size you'd see if you had ordered some old-timey phone booths from England and had them shipped to your house.

The boxes had wheels and, when empty, a single person (or a married person) could move them rather easily. When full, it took two. The boxes went up a ramp and into a midsized moving truck, where they were stored during the week. The lock on the truck often froze. Thus, the truck cab included a lighter, and someone got the very cool job of holding the lighter on the lock until it warmed up enough to pop open with the key. The whole thing seemed like a scene from a heist movie.

Each Sunday, the boxes were rolled up to the stage area. All the cords and speakers and stands were unloaded and set in place. Then the super useful but not very attractive boxes were rolled out of sight until after the service, when the system reversed: The full boxes were grudgingly rolled back up the ramp and into the truck. (The boxes grudged, not the willing volunteers.)

Casters work like a charm on empty things. On full things, it's more of a gamble.

We rolled the boxes down the school hallway, and it's important to note just how big these boxes were. They were about as tall as they were wide, and they barely fit through the double doors of the school gym. They were so tall, in fact, that an emergency fire sprinkler head was broken clean off by one.

Ever wonder what happens when an emergency fire sprinkler head is broken clean off?

Here's what happens: Water pours out. Lots and lots of water. And not nice water. This water has been sitting in the pipes since the last fire, which was never, so it just sat there growing smelly stuff. Now, glad to be out in the open, it poured like a stallion herd that discovered an opening in the corral, but it smelled much worse. Also, the fire alarm went off.

When this happens, someone must call the fire department and report, "No fire." But as it turns out, the fire chief still has to come out. Most fire chiefs have a red SUV, which is not as cool as the big ol' hook-and-ladder rigs. Maybe for this reason, or maybe for personal reasons, the fire chief was not glad to come out to see us.

He looked at the water, which was quickly filling a full-size waste bin. He sniffed the water and looked at us as if we had intentionally let him down. His expression said, *I have given you so many chances, and you just didn't live up to your potential. I am not angry. I am just disappointed. And also angry!*

I couldn't help thinking, *Dude! Your whole job is to prevent fire, and no fire happened here. You nailed it. Why can't you just be happy you are not doing your job?* I don't think I understand fire chiefs.

Shortly after that, the church bought some land because that's what churches do. They grow up and leave the rental nest, flying into the uncharted air of property development. Then some other things happened that don't fit the metaphor as well, because that's how metaphors work.

# 41

# Guest Preaching for Fun and (Rarely) Profit

Of all the kinds of preaching you can do, guest preaching is the best. "Why?" you ask. And I could reply, "Why don't you just believe me? What's wrong with you—no, what's wrong with *us*? Where did we all go wrong?"

Or I could just explain.

When you're guest preaching you are, by definition, not going to be there long. You're probably leaving right after the benediction. This means you can say whatever you want. Want to singe raised eyebrows by slamming adultery? Go all King David on them. Then just drive away! It's not your problem what may or may not have happened between the parishioners. You are already gone.

At some point in a career, every preacher wants to preach against coveting. We live in a materialistic society. It's been that way since materials were invented. But you can't slam your own congregation and then pass the offering plate. It just doesn't add up, so to speak. As a guest preacher, on the other hand, you can rail against money in all its evil forms. It's easy and fun!

My dad had a standard "traveling sermon" I heard so often I could preach it myself by the time I was ten. He'd open with the question Jesus asks in Matthew 16:13: "Who do people say that the Son of Man is?" There are three answers, and there you have your three points. Then the passage wraps up with an application that practically applies itself. Easy.

We would hear this sermon on vacation, when the local preacher was glad to have a morning off. We'd hear it at Grandma's church whenever Dad headed that way. And we'd hear it at nearby churches whenever they did one of those crazy "We're trading preachers!" Sundays.

About one generation later, word got around that I, like my dad, could drive and preach. (But not at the same time.) My go-to message also had three points because if we, as a church people, believe anything, it's that sermons have three points. Mine came from Psalm 46:10, and it was simplicity itself: "Be still, and know that I am God." It was God's message to His Old Testament people, and it still applies seamlessly today.

1. *Be still.* Our lives are crazy. We go at a pace that kills us toward goals that also kill us. We need to slow down.

2. *And know.* Doubt is the fuel that keeps us running at the aforementioned crazy pace. But if we slow down enough to hear the still, small voice of God, we can know that God is with us.

3. *That I am God.* Your job isn't God, your lawn isn't God, and getting your kid into a good college isn't God. God is God. If you can be still, then you can know this.

See? The message practically preaches itself, and I never copyrighted it. Take it if you'd like. I used this thing everywhere, and I'd use it again.

I never asked for money. That just didn't seem right. And when I was done preaching, the congregation usually agreed with that assessment. Sometimes I would get a "love offering," which sounds like it ought to be candy or flowers. Usually, it was a restaurant gift card. One church gave me 100 dollars a pop, and I preached there a half dozen times. It was always great. Except that I opened with my traveling sermon, so I had to come up with something new on subsequent visits.

That's the trouble with easy-to-preach sermons. There's a chance somebody will actually remember them.

# 42

# Hallmark of My Career

Monday through Friday for more than 30 years now, I've worked at Hallmark, the card company. We do lots more than cards now, but when I started, cards were our bread and butter. Also the protein, if you want to take the saying to its logical conclusion.

The main office is a big campus in downtown Kansas City, on the Missouri side. Kansas City has a Missouri side and a Kansas side, which exist, as far as I can tell, for two reasons.

1.  So that the local news channels can run, "Which side costs more to live on?" investigations every few years. Turns out to be about the same. You pay for this on one side, for that on the other.

2.  If you live in Kansas and work in Missouri, you get the opportunity to help out both sides when you pay taxes. This is where it turns out to be super helpful to marry someone who is good at math, which I did (but my wife did not). Lana has tried to explain the taxes to me. I've concluded that they are impossible to understand. I don't think I'm missing much, and so far I have not gone to jail.

Most of the time, I write humor for Hallmark. To be honest, I can't help myself. When I've been accidentally assigned to write something serious, I get feedback like "Too funny." Conversely, I can write humor on purpose and hear "Not funny enough."

The thing most people want to know about writing cards is this: "How do you think of your ideas?" If I knew, I would tell you, but it's still kind of a mystery to me. I sit at my desk, convinced I'm a fraud. I will soon be discovered and exposed as such. Guys in jumpsuits will come for my computer. They'll escort me from the building. Later, they'll repossess the house and the car.

The fear drives me, I suppose, and I make fun of it. And everything else. For me, the basic premise of card-writing has always been, "We are friends, and I want to recognize your birthday in a way that will strengthen that friendship through shared laughter." Or something close to that. So that part has not changed in 30 years. Nor had it changed in the 30 before that—nor will it change during the 30 years to come.

What has changed is what we in the industry call "subject matter." We call it that because it sounds more impressive than "stuff." It's stuff, though. Stuff you and your birthday-having friend talk about, comment on, recognize, and share. If we can make some of that stuff into a card that also says "Happy Birthday," well, there's my career right there.

At Hallmark, we have writers who have been alive for fewer years than I've been at the job. Isn't that weird? Hallmark really does have that kind of big-family atmosphere. It's not uncommon to find employees who have been employed for more than four decades. It's a lot of happy birthdays, and I've been fortunate enough to see lots of my cards printed. At first, I'd go to the card shop and hang around, spying on shoppers. Once while doing this, I saw someone buy one of my first cards! My wife was with me, and she started to run toward the person to hug them and tell them that the author of their card was available for autographs. I was able to stop her before security was summoned.

Over the years I've met a few other former pastors of various stripes who were writing or editing cards. I'm not sure how that works. Lot of former pastors go into life insurance. That one's a little clearer. As a pastor, you're already kind of insuring life, the "more abundantly" kind. Then you just expand that to offer term or whole.

Maybe what writing cards has in common with the clerical calling is that both jobs want people to be closer to each other, to enjoy their blessings more intentionally, and to be more conscious of the things that draw us all together. Or maybe it's that we like to sit around talking, and you have to do something to pay the bills. But I think it's mostly the other things I have mentioned.

Making jokes has come naturally to me for as long as I can remember.

But I have no idea when they are going to be *good* jokes, especially good jokes that are different from the previous ones I have written.

But there are presses that need to print the jokes, and trucks that need to ship the jokes, and stores that need to sell the jokes. A lot is riding on the work we writers do. That's where the tension comes in. Not a bad kind of tension but the kind I heard one time compared to a guitar string. Too little tension, and it's just a thud. Too much tension, and it snaps. But when the tension is just right? Well, that's music.

While that's a lovely metaphor, it's small comfort when you're sitting at your desk trying to think of the millionth way to say "Happy Birthday."

Each writer does it differently. What works for me would not work for them. Sometimes, what worked for me doesn't *work* for me anymore. When that happens, it's nice to have the internet.

I look up the ten-day weather forecast. I look up the week's menu in the employee cafeteria. I look up which movies are opening the next weekend. I look up grandkids' pictures on Instagram. I look up lots of random stuff. Time is killed.

Now, with less time available, I get serious about writing humor. And once I've done what I tell myself is a reasonable amount and/or the clock says it's time to go home, well, I try to stop thinking about work. And I usually can.

Sometimes that's made easier by thinking about vacations.

# 43

# The Bahamas

One of the really great things about a full-time job that *isn't* being a youth minister is that there's vacation time, and there's enough money to go somewhere on vacation. Both of these ideas were new concepts to me in the mid-1980s.

Our family had been on maybe two trips that you'd call proper vacations. Otherwise it was mostly visiting one grandparent or the other and hoping some cousins near your age would be there.

Preachers did not get a lot of time off, and they didn't get a lot of money to spend when they had time. We Hallmark greeting card writers don't get what you'd call Scrooge McDuck rich, but we do okay. And we get vacation time.

We had just bought our first house, and again, this was the mid-1980s. They were not just giving houses away like they would in a few years, creating a national crisis. No, when we got that house, you had to prove you had a job—and would most likely keep the job. Further, your body contained several healthy internal organs that the bank could come for if you missed a payment.

Our first house was modest. It was a split of some kind—I've never been clear on how that works. Was it front to back? Side to side? In to out? Can't tell you. It was split some way.

We walked through the house with the builder before it was finished and removed a coat closet and a bunch of canister lights so we could get it down to the lowest price possible. As I said, it was modest. But much nicer than the apartment that came with a free dead mouse! And it was even nicer than the house in New Mexico.

Building the house was stressful, though, in that way where you don't realize you're stressed until you realize you keep trying to head for bed at 7:30 and you're frequently pouring chocolate sauce directly into your mouth.

So we went to a travel agent, which is what everybody did BC (before cell phones) and said, "We have X amount of money. How far can we get?" Turned out that the answer was…the Bahamas.

Having never left the continent, my wife and I both thought this sounded exotic and fancy and beachy. We were all for it. Also, not to get too detailed, but we had a house now and had started thinking about filling up the bedrooms. With kids, I mean. But also with furniture. So we headed for the Bahamas, looking forward to the time of our lives.

We totally nailed this vacation. Again, not to get too detailed, but my wife came back from the fancy international airplane bathroom and told me, "We are not starting a family this week."

We could still shop for furniture, but no kids for the rooms yet.

Disclaimer: The following stuff happened 30 years ago, and maybe the Bahamas are super awesome now. And in fact, they were probably pretty awesome then too. For other people.

The airport was basically a tin shed that somehow conveyed an air of abject sadness, even as the sun shone and the sea birds cawed—if that's the sound a sea bird makes. We had been there about an hour when I asked when I could start making fun of it.

"Not yet," I was firmly informed.

Our hotel room was okay. It had a tremendous view of lots of other rooms just like it. We were on the inside of a horseshoe shape and, mirror-like, were looking right at our own hotel. Donning our brand-new and totally unnecessary-in-Kansas swimsuits, we ran into the ocean. Then my wife quickly ran right back out, covered in hives. I was still not allowed to make fun yet.

And guess what? The hotel was making improvements! Guess when? All day long. Hammers hammered and drills drilled and generators generated. You could hear the progress everywhere! Good for them!

The walls grew mold. We asked about it and were told that it had to do with being near the ocean. This was about the time my wife gave me clearance to mock.

We had a sheaf of buy-one, get-one coupons that had come with our travel package. We went to one dinner using them. That took up our disposable income. BOGO only works if you can afford to BO. There's no GO if you can't BO. The mocking gates were open now, and mocking flowed freely.

TV was free, and it began about ten o'clock each night. Deciding to stay up as long as possible so that we could sleep on the beach to kill the remaining days, we began to watch an old movie. It was the one where Chevy Chase goes on, you guessed it, vacation! The irony made us laugh and laugh. Then the power went out, and the entire hotel went black. We fell asleep chuckling and slept soundly till about two o'clock, when the TV and the lights blared back on.

Six hours later, we went to the front desk and asked if we could go home early. We were directed to a small office where a stern woman told us that we could leave the next day if we paid an extra 75 dollars—and we'd get none of our original deposit back. We were openly laughing now. The lady in the small office had no idea why.

A cruise ship cruised by the sliver of ocean we could see from inside the horseshoe and blew its crazy-loud horn. The people who waved from the railing looked so outrageously happy that it was just heartbreaking.

In the postmortem discussion of this vacation, we decided we were maybe 100 dollars a day from having an okay time. It might as well have been 1,000 dollars. We felt guilty enough about going to the Bahamas. No sense trying it again for much more money.

However, a few years later, we went on a cruise. Those people on that Bahamian cruise ship weren't faking. We now know they were having the time of their lives.

# 44

# Needle Phobia

Have you heard of those people who go on mission trips to places in the world where they need to get shots first? Are you, perhaps, one of those people? If so, God bless you, for two reasons.

1. You're doing important work, being the "hands and feet" of Jesus in places where that's needed the most.
2. No way am I doing that work. Because of the shots.

My earliest memories of doctor visits include me saying, "Don't want a shot, don't want a shot!" My first pediatrician, which sounds like a fun kids' game but isn't, was in the town next to one of my childhood homes, and there was a big hill on the way. At the top of said hill, I'd begin imploring in a polite, and increasingly desperate, way to avoid going "under the needle." I'm not sure that's what the expression means, but I don't care.

*Phobia* comes from the Greek word meaning, "This is going to hurt." Telling children that shots don't hurt is one of the earliest lies adults foist on children. Santa, the Tooth Fairy, and bullies-are-really-scared-on-the-inside have *nothing* on "Shots don't hurt." Because they hurt a little, no matter what, but where they really stick you (painfully accurate pun intended) is in your mind.

Blessed with a good imagination, I began thinking about the shot a couple of miles from the doctor's chamber of horror. And as my imagination developed, so did the amount of time I was able to get queasy. I could have a dream about getting a shot and wake up chilled and not able to go back to sleep. That was last week.

When I went to get blood drawn to get married I aodsifhds vo7iluyr3 uepofjdvm…THUD!

Ha-ha! Just kidding. I didn't really pass out just thinking about getting my blood drawn. Here's what happened. The nurse saw I was the same color as the paper form I'd just filled out. She asked if I'd like to sit on the weird and creepy bed/table thing. I said I was fine and then slumped into a sitting position on the creepy bed/table. She asked if I'd like to, perhaps, lie down. Again I said I was fine. Then I kind of fell over onto the creepy bed/table. A few minutes later, I was apparently street-legal to get married and had not aodsifhds vo7iluyr3 uepofjdvm…THUD!

Ha-ha, another hilarious joke where I don't really pass out.

Both of our kids were C-section births. At first, I thought this meant I would be unable to witness the birth from the more-desired A or B sections. I wasn't sure whether to be offended or relieved. But, as it turned out, I watched both kids come into the world, without having to temporarily leave it myself. Yes, they do a lot of things that are pretty serious in a C-section delivery, but at least me getting a shot was not part of it.

However, the day after each birth, a guy came into the room with an adorable little carrying case of vials and he aodsifhds vo7iluyr3 uepofjdvm…THUD!

Okay, *that* time I really did pass out.

# 45

# Surefire Parenting Tips from Me, the Expert

Tip number 1: If anyone ever tells you, "I have surefire parenting tips. I am an expert," then you should ignore that person. And if you want to ignore *that*, the advice I just gave, you are probably making another smart move.

We raised two nearly flawless children, Riley and Paige. When people have questions about them, I make up answers that sound reasonable. Meanwhile, my wife answers with an authority that sounds foreign to me. If you had raised Riley and Paige, they probably would have come out nearly flawless for you as well.

But what about your actual kids? No offense (I don't know your kids), but good luck. Today's parents have a really tough row to hoe. You know a job is hard when it can be referenced via farming metaphors.

Easy things get "piece of cake!" or "like butter!" That's because there is nothing challenging at stake with cake or butter. Farming seems really hard, as does raising any kids who are not my kids. And, as I just mentioned, mine are already raised.

Raising nearly flawless children is kind of a pain, though, to tell the truth. Other people—friends from work, friends from church, neighbors, and teachers in elementary, middle, and high school—are having a tough time to hear them tell it. My wife and I have learned to *almost* lie with our facial expressions. When a fellow parent says, "I just can't get Geoffrey to stop setting the sofa on fire," we nod sagely and make empathetic sounds. The truth, of course, is that I am very scared of Geoffrey. I would not be able to sleep in the same house with him, especially on the sofa.

When another parent confides, "Brittany just won't stop robbing liquor stores, and we're really worried about what will happen once she's old enough to drive," we again try to look unhorrified. But we're pretty horrified, and also very, very glad that the biggest challenges our kids ever gave us were not big at all.

If your kids are/were also nearly flawless, we could talk a long time, and I have promised my wife I would not try to one-up you, even though I'm pretty sure I could. See how easy that is? And how bad it sounds? Now that I think of it, our nearly flawless children put us in an untenable position. They're the worst, just like everyone else's.

They came of age during the reign of minivans, and I am very glad of it. SUVs are all the rage now. You're probably reading this chapter in an SUV while you wait for a kid to emerge from some sort of practice or rehearsal or playdate, but you're really missing out if you have kids and don't have a van.

In a van, the kids are so far away! It's like magic. It's almost like they're in another car, but you don't have to pay for that one. Don't worry. Soon you'll be paying for more cars than you ever thought possible, but for now, when the kids are vanned up, it's almost as if they're in another room. Or, if they're very small, you can put the car seat in a spot that's pretty close and still have your own space, called the captain's chair.

You don't get a captain's chair anywhere else. So get a van. That's parenting tip number 2, and if you want to ignore *that*, as I said before, "Good luck."

# 46

# Soccer Dad

Some parents, especially dads, tend to live vicariously through the sports achievements of their children, especially their sons. As you can read elsewhere in this book, my personal collegiate soccer achievements did not leave a lot to live up to. We won one game, by forfeit, and I once very nearly broke my fibula on a guy. He was a very big, very fast guy, and it was quite clear he was about to score yet another goal on our beleaguered team.

In an attempt to stop that, I swung my leg at him as he ran by. The front of my leg hit his very-fast-moving upper body, and for a minute we were looking right at each other as the rest of his body rose into the air. He flew for what seemed like three or four feet and then landed just about the time the ref blew the whistle. Turns out you can't just kick an opposing player. He was fine. I suffered what's called a "bone bruise" by guys who most certainly were not doctors and had no idea. It hurt for a year and was purple for about that long. Twelve months. I'm lucky the guy wasn't bigger. He would have broken my leg for sure.

So the bar for my son was pretty low when he took the field, and I can say with confidence that we were not good sports parents. Oh, we sliced the oranges, and we pooled the players in our van (vans are the best!), but we just counted the minutes until each game ended. It might have been more fun if we'd had some money on it, but that's probably illegal.

Then again, the thrill of breaking the law to bet on under-12 soccer is probably part of the appeal. And it for sure would have been more fun if any of the games had been played when the games were scheduled. Instead, we had one entire season in which each game was rained out and then played later. And they play soccer in regular rain. This was lightning-storm rain, and it affected every game. You never knew when something you hated would be rescheduled—so that you could hate it later, at a much less convenient time.

Unless it was forfeited entirely. One of those blessed events happened that season. In fact, I made it happen.

Under-12 soccer is not a majestic game. It's mostly a scramble, a jumble, or some other kind of old-time game that doesn't look like much on the field. A couple of kids usually stand out as clearly gifted and move up and down the field like gazelles who care about sports. Our son was not one of these. He was fine, but we were still saving for college, if you know what I'm saying.

During one rescheduled game, either just before or just after the half-time orange-slice break, the 22 under-12s were in a scrum at midfield when a kid from the other team loaded up and slammed a great, solid, very hard kick that sent the ball about three feet and right into our son's eye. We knew it was his eye by the way he yelled, "My eye!" and covered it with both hands before hitting the ground.

I went out to see if he was okay. Does that sound like a calamitous sentence? If you know your under-12 soccer, it does. And now you're shaking your head in a justifiably judgmental manner.

See, parents, unless they are coaches, are not allowed on the field. Ever. This is actually a very good rule, which I support. This was before the helicopter-parent years, but it foretold such a time. The rule was in place for the protection of the refs, who were just barely over-12s themselves and not keen to argue with adult parents acting like kids over penalty calls.

But this was an eye, and it struck me as a bigger deal. The ref, whom I put at about 15, stood in front of me and said, "You can't be here." I didn't pay any attention and walked around him and out to midfield, where my son was still on the ground, holding his face where, fortunately, his eye still resided.

Game over. Our team lost. We went home and waited for the next game to be rescheduled.

A couple of soccer moms and I went to a district office to talk about it a week later, but when the league official walked in wearing those black gym shoes and whistle on a lanyard, I saw the writing on the office wall. No recourse, just another apology from me to 15-year-old refs everywhere—and a deep, abiding sense of gratitude when our son gave up sports for music.

# 47

# Band Dad

My son traded the soccer field for the marching band, where he played the bass. You're probably wondering how the massive bass moves down the football field at halftime or Main Street in a parade, but fret not. He played the *electric* bass, so he simply plugged in his instrument and plunked away, standing next to a speaker.

Later, he became a drum major, and things became a lot more complicated.

Drum majors are the people who lead the band. On game days, or for band competitions, the drum major stands on an aluminum platform, hoping fervently there isn't a lightning storm. The stands are moved into place by helpful volunteers, and those volunteers are collectively referred to as Band Dads. There were also Band Moms, and they seemed to be having fun. I don't know for sure. I was never invited to any of their meetings. But we Band Dads were not a fun group, probably because we were composed exclusively of guys.

Guys have very strict rules, regulations, bylaws, and codes. The tough part of these strictures and structures is that none of them are written down. They are expressed with a series of looks and almost imperceptible head nods. Any group of dads, no matter how loosely formed, will soon elect an Alpha. This guy will be in charge of whatever happens next, even if that's just deciding that there's nothing to do and it's okay to go home. The Alpha won't be officially elected. He'll just assume the role by being guy who owns the most tools. Or driving the truck with the most options and/or hauling capacity. Hauling capacity is a huge thing for dads, even if they are never, ever going to haul anything.

The way to distinguish an Alpha is simple. I disclose it here for perhaps the first time, so pay attention. When any group or organization asks for volunteers, there's a deer-in-the-headlights moment that can go on for a long time. Then, finally, one man steps forward. That man is the Alpha. On the rare occurrence of two dads stepping forward simultaneously, they must take ten paces apart and then run toward each other, ramming their heads together. The dad who remains standing wins. This is also why you almost never see two dads step forward.

I was nothing like an Alpha Band Dad. I found the easiest job: carrying a hollow-tubed aluminum platform to a spot and putting it down. Later, I would pick it back up when I received the signal. (My son stepping down from the platform.)

Then the platform was set sideways on a trailer and returned to the bus garage to wait for the next assignment. I got to ride on the trailer, wind in my hair, smile on my face, knowing I had done the absolute minimum.

I also got to do one very cool thing. The band my son directed was very, very good, and they had a teacher/director/coach/Ultimate Alpha who was very aggressive. He secured an invitation for the band to play a parade in New York. And not Ithaca, either. The real one, the one from the movies. I got to be a sponsor.

Being a sponsor (there were six of us) meant you were given charge of a group of high-strung kids who were to be unleashed upon the city. While most of our high schoolers were, for the most part, well-behaved Midwesterners who were a bit cowed by the big city, a few musicians tended to wander off, and we had to corral them. But in the end, everyone who departed from Kansas returned to Kansas. Thus, the trip was a success. Yes, one magical New York-in-a-movie thing happened, but it didn't happen to a teen. It happened to me.

For some reason, I got separated from my charges for a few minutes while we toured Chinatown. It began to rain. Do the people who run New York make it rain during a crisis just to make things more cinematic?

I didn't have an umbrella, but all the locals did. As I walked along, somewhat taller than the average person of Chinese heritage, one of them held up his umbrella for me. Then the next person did. I walked past him, and the next person raised an umbrella, and the next, and the next. From above, I'm certain it looked like I was walking along those four or five blocks in a movie about the city where...something happens.

Do I miss being a Band Dad? The pounding of the drums, the trill of the whistles, the wind whipping across the open trailer? No, no I don't. Not at all.

But I kind of miss being in a movie in Chinatown.

# 48

# Cello There!

I was secretly thrilled when my daughter decided she wanted to play the cello. As we have just learned, her older brother already played the upright bass, the largest (by volume) instrument your musically inclined child can choose. Does the tuba weigh more? Of course it does, but it's a sedan compared to the 16-wheeler that is the upright bass. Drums are worse, that's for sure. Drums come in roughly one million pieces, and there is a literal key you can lose. Any kid thing that includes a key that can be lost? Well, there's no cliché about this because everyone inherently understands the impending disaster. But at least the drums do come apart. The bass is like an atom. Or a nucleus? Whatever it is that cannot be split into smaller pieces. Except, of course, a bass is huge.

So I was happy with the cello for the above reasons. But also because it meant orchestra, and orchestra meant classical music. Classical music is like flossing or eating vegetables. You know you should do it daily, but to be honest, you do it right before the checkup. I thought the cello would make me appreciate classical music. After that, who knew? Maybe I'd read Shakespeare in the original language it was written in. Maybe I'd paint still-life fruit paintings. Maybe I'd go to the ballet, and not just the one about the Christmas nutcracker. The possibilities were endless.

But they ended pretty quickly. I bought the kids a CD of musicians who played cool songs on stringed instruments that were not guitars. They listened politely, maybe once, and not all the way through.

We did not become close with the other orchestra parents. We did not eat fancy cheeses with them. Were they even eating fancy cheeses? I have no idea. Not with us, at any rate.

Not joining some kind of fancy-cheese-eating club was bad enough. The other bad thing about orchestra was the strange and heartless system whereby members competed for chairs. Not because the school district couldn't afford chairs. That happened only with books. The budding musicians competed for first chair and then the chairs after that. This struck me, and still does, as antithetical to the idea of making music in the first place. The jazz band, where our son played bass, seemed like a cool, underground club where everyone wanted everyone else to have fun. But orchestra was a blood sport. It was like finding out the math club had started arm wrestling for money. Weird.

Today, Paige just plays cello for fun, or sometimes for weddings, or sometimes at a church I have not attended. But I'll bet that church is super fancy and sophisticated and probably breaking new ground in the area of high-end cheese.

# 49

# The Perfect Sofa

I have the perfect sofa. I've had it for a long time. Sadly, it exists only in my mind. Sofa, couch, davenport. Call it what you will. It will never materialize for me. But let me tell you about it.

It's made of leather, but no sad-eyed cows were harmed.

It's firm but soft.

It's perfectly weathered and aged, yet it looks brand new.

It's timeless but very cutting edge.

You can lie on it and sleep like a baby. You can sit on it and sit like a...baby who can sit up and is really comfortable on this awesome, currently imaginary couch.

How much would such a sofa cost, you ask? The perfect amount. Not so cheap that it does not somehow symbolize the hard work and dumb luck and outright blessed blessings of a lifetime, but not so much that it's a moral issue.

So far, I've missed by not shooting high enough when it comes to couches. I've spent more than college-age me ever thought a couch could cost and still not achieved it. And not once, mind you, but more like a half dozen times.

There's one miss currently residing in my son's living room. There's a miss in my basement, where it silently mocks me, saying, "Yes, this was a furniture fail, but go upstairs and you know what? There's an even bigger one."

Leather sofas have been donated to (super fun!) youth group rooms and picked up and taken away by mission organizations that had a truck. Other sofas have been garage-sold in garage sales to raise money to go to Guatemala.

Don't think they didn't come with matching love seats. They did. That just makes it worse.

I think a lot of us who grew up tithing our first allowance have this issue, whether with a sofa, car, house, or horse. Seriously, I know people who have horses. Plural. And boats and other houses besides the house they live in most of the time. I knew some people who had a room they never went into. They were "keeping it perfect" because it had been pictured in a magazine.

And I know other people who aren't sure they can stay in their apartment but have no idea where else they'd go.

We were taught that tithing would take care of problems like this. But then there were love offerings and building fund drives and camps and colleges and conventions and other things that did not start with "c" but still required money. It's not easy to figure out how much to give away and how much to keep.

Every now and then a preacher or an author will mention that Old Testament tithing actually required much more giving, maybe up to 30 percent of one's income. Not surprisingly, these preachers and books are not very popular.

Even now, I can sense a general squirming. We just don't like to talk about money. My parents, after the ten-percent talk, hardly mentioned it at all.

A certain amount of money was set aside for school clothes at the start of each year, and one year I wanted an upgrade. Not to name names, but the jeans the budget called for had "Tough Skins," if you know what I'm saying. However, I wanted ones that were more Lee Vise. So, I used 90 percent of the allowance money I had left over for the upcharge, and it seemed to work out fine.

I'd be lying if I said that settled it and now I'm perfectly content with the contents of my bank account. It still kind of kills me a little to go to a full-price movie when I know there's a half-price option on Saturday morning. And I am truly happy when eating an appetizer that is being marketed as part of an entire hour of happy—and therefore costs half as much.

But the perfect sofa is out there. I'll always be looking out of the corner of my eye for it, like an upholstered Moby Dick, wherever fine furniture is offered. And it's going to cost more than I think it should. Will

I finally buy it, once I find it? Probably not. I'll probably get a "pretty close" option and give away the one in the basement and move the one that's upstairs downstairs, like on a British TV show about social norms. Watch for that basement couch at a youth group garage sale near you. It's really a pretty nice couch!

# 50

# Two Weddings and No Funerals (So Far)

Nowadays, anybody can perform a wedding. In the olden times, you had to be ordained, which means a church had to recognize you and, usually in a special ceremony, "set you aside" for doing church stuff.

Today, anybody with an active email address can get ordained enough to tie a knot. Even though I didn't do any weddings as a paid staff member at a church, I've done lots and lots since then. How many? Not sure. A couple dozen? A score? They have mostly been for friends, and recently for marriageable-aged kids of friends.

I did two weddings as a pro, and it was…interesting, but not for me. First, I don't see how anyone makes a living at it. The most money I ever got, times 52 weekends, wouldn't buy an economy car, and there's no way anyone is doing weddings 52 weekends a year. You could double up sometimes, sure, but that still wouldn't yield a living wage. And it feels kind of weird too. As more and more people move around or don't identify with a specific local church for life—as they used to—it's less likely your wedding is going to be done in your "home" church by whomever is pastor at the time. So that's where the weddings-as-business thing comes in. But to me, it always feels like doing something for money that I ought to be doing for free, like helping a friend move or tossing the neighbor's wayward cat back over the fence.

Anyway, one of the weddings was unlike any of the others I have conducted. This one involved a Peruvian Tribunal. (Believe me, I take any and all opportunities to reference Peruvian Tribunals.)

A friend was trying to start a wedding planning business, which of course wasn't a twinkle in capitalism's eye when I got married. She had a client, a lovely middle-aged woman from Peru who was living in Kansas at the time because that's the part of America that's the most similar to Peru.

She met a lovely middle-aged American guy. Eventually, they decided to marry.

But there was a problem. This woman had already been married back in Peru, about a decade prior. That marriage was over now, and life had moved on. But the woman's former church had not moved on. Technically, they had to disallow the old marriage before the woman could embark on a new one.

I know this sounds weird for those of us not wedded in a Peruvian church, but when you think about it, you don't go to your new job and also have to put in an appearance at your old job from time to time. You don't begin high school but still drop by middle school every third Thursday. So I kind of understand the problem.

The folks in Peru who officially delegitimize one's nuptials are called a Tribunal. I assume this is because there are three of them and they wear hats with three points—and they sit at a three-sided table. They do lots of other secret stuff, all involving three or multiples of three.

Regardless of what they wear when they convene, they share their decisions only by mail. They are old-school, the Peruvian Tribunals, and you can't really push back because there are three of them and only one of you. What are *you* gonna do?

At the rehearsal for the wedding, I'm standing there, and a priest is standing there, and if the mail doesn't come the next morning, well, I'm the guy. If a carrier pigeon or bicycle messenger or something shows up with an envelope, I get only half my modest fee—but my Saturday is freed up.

Turned out I got my entire modest fee. It was all me, all the time, with a grouchy priest in the third row, scowling at me a little.

The bride brought international complications to the special day, but the groom had something up his rented sleeve as well.

He told me he had a special surprise for his intended. I was under strict orders not to tell her. Also, I was not supposed to call attention to a large tarp thrown over something near the front of the outdoor space where we held the wedding.

The couple finished reading vows they had written for each other, which were pretty good, though not as funny as they would have been if I had helped. Then the groom gave me a furtive nod and began to head toward the tarp.

His bride, not knowing what was going on, held on even tighter to his hands, perhaps having lost a husband this way back in Peru. He tugged; she dug in. Finally, I said to her, "You have to let him go."

She did. He walked over to the tarp, dramatically swept it aside, and there was a keyboard and a music stand! What? The bride and I were both surprised by this, and we looked expectantly at him. One of us began to cry softly.

Then he played and sang. A song. I don't remember what it was. It was some sort of popular love ballad kind of thing, one you could have heard on the radio on your way to the wedding. The trouble with that is that everyone in attendance had probably heard that song performed really well. And this was not really well. This was not even *well*. One of us began to cry harder, and at least one of us probably took a moment to wonder about the Peruvian Tribunal and how they decide whatever they decide.

. . . . . . . . . . . .

I also did a wedding for a groom I had known most of his life. He was one of my son's best friends. While my son and this groom are both smart kids in their own right, together, they became very dangerously stupid. Every once in a while, we'll find out random details of sleepovers that nearly ended in explosions or drownings or arrests. And those are just the ones we've heard about.

The parents of this daredevil groom were friends as well. That's going to matter in a minute.

The couple got married in Lexington or possibly Louisville, Kentucky. When you know the names of only two towns in a state, and they sound kind of similar, well, those names are interchangeable.

Louisville (or possibly Lexington) is a beautiful place. Hills roll, horses gallop, and fences stretch as far as the eye can see. It's a lovely place for a wedding, and the bride had a perfect outdoor venue—in view of a castle built by one of those rich crazy people who build castles in places like Lexington, or possibly Louisville.

The event would have been scenic as can be, but a storm was coming. Not the way they talk about the years leading up to World War I in a documentary. This was an *actual* storm. Cell phones had just become popular, and people were watching the radar reports. Power went out in either Lexington or Louisville, and we knew the storm was headed right for whichever town we were in.

That wedding started on time, maybe even a tad early. There's usually a little leeway in starting times—let the stragglers straggle a bit. Not this time. Grandmas got seated with an alacrity they had not shown in years. My daughter was playing cello for the processional, and she proceeded at a brisk, non-cello pace as the wind picked up her sheet music and sent it into the pasture.

The bride was going to appear in a white horse-drawn carriage, but horses are smart. The trainer, the wedding planner, and various helpful guests could not get the horse to walk forward into what it knew, even without a smartphone, was the teeth of a storm. After a few hesitant clip-clops of horse hooves, the bride scrambled out of the carriage and kind of walked/ran toward the front. She stood there, shivering, as her veil stood straight out like a weather vane, ironically. Rain began to fall.

The parents of the couple were, of course, sitting right in front. I asked them if it was okay if we did this really fast. Fearing for their lives, they said, "Sure." The rain intensified.

I asked the bride if she "did." She said, "I do." I asked the groom if he did. He said he did too. I said, "Y'all are married now." The y'all was thrown in as a nod to Lexington or Louisville.

Then I realized I was holding a live mic in a lightning storm, and the rain was whipping sideways now. The last thing I said into that little lightning rod in my hand was, "*Save yourselves!*" Then we all ran inside.

Rain pounded the building. Lightning flashed. Thunder shook that venue to its trendy, rough-hewn foundations.

Then it all stopped. The sun came out. Magnificent rainbows formed, and some of the best wedding pictures ever were snapped. Nice place for a wedding—Louisville. (Or possibly Lexington.)

# 51

# Word Play

People get married for all kinds of reasons. The best one being that you can't imagine life without your intended, and you intend to live happily ever after, together.

Some other things come along with that, and one of them is that the person you married can tell you when your mind is working differently than the minds of other people. Apparently, my mind does that all the time.

For example, I apparently can't hear words the way everyone who is normal hears words. I have to think about what they mean and where they came from and how they're being used now compared to how they have been used historically—and the variables for gender, socioeconomic status, and region. It's a lot to process.

- "Float a check," "bounce a check," "check kiting." To me, these words make it sound like checks are the absolute most fun things you can have! Every kid should have a big stack of checks he or she can bounce and float and fly on a windy day! Yay, checks!

- "Double-edged sword." Why is this always a negative warning? "Careful, that's a double-edged sword." I have never sword-fought, but if I were to sword-fight, I would very much prefer to have a sword with twice as many edges as my opponent's. If there were a triple-edged sword, that would be even better.

- "Painting with a broad brush." My wife hits me with this one all the time. When she does, I secretly high-five myself and think, *Argument won!* Because a broad brush would so obviously be the best kind of brush for painting. I want to get any and all painting over with as soon as possible, and the broader the brush, the better. Strangely, though, every time I've secretly thought, *Argument won!* it turns out the argument was not won, secretly or otherwise.

- "Thrown under the bus." How many times did this happen before it became an expression? Even once is a felony, right? And I think the throw-ee pretty much dies. I don't think anyone has ever said, "What a rough flight from Atlanta! I feel as though I have been thrown under a bus!" It's usually more like, "Tina blamed me for not bringing a big enough punch bowl. Way to throw me under the bus!" I don't think anyone who has ever been thrown under a bus is around to compare any social slight to it. Which brings us to...

- "Throw the baby out with the bathwater." How many babies were thrown out before this became a saying? "Where's Trevor?" "Oh, no! Not again! We have to stop bathing our babies so carelessly!"

- "Kingpin." Why is this never a good title? No one is the high-way clean-up crew kingpin. It's always about crime. I don't know how pins choose a king, but would they consistently choose criminals? Or is it ancestral? Was your dad the king of pins, so now you are? If so, was he a criminal? Weird.

- "Big cheese." Also used for crime, but in other ways too. You could be the big cheese of the highway clean-up crew, but why? Why would the *size* of cheese mean anything? It sounds like the cheese chose to be big instead of just being made that way by the...cheesemonger? And no group would name themselves "mongers." That moniker very clearly came from somewhere else.

Don't think I can't do this all day. Because I promise you I can. And I never take Sundays off.

- "Narthex," "foyer," "front part of the building?" Why so many options?

- Is *anything* "held in readiness" that isn't a hymn at the end of a service?

- "Poor as a church mouse?" Are there wealthy church mice? Middle-class mice, maybe?

- Why is it only "fellowship" when it's all Christians? When you're working with your neighbors on the Highway Clean-Up Crew, isn't that fellowship?

See? My mind works like this all the time. I'm not choosing to wonder. I literally cannot stop wondering. And then I wonder about *that*. It's a good thing I have a wife who will tell me when I'm not being normal. It's an even better thing she doesn't seem to mind my mind.

# 52

# Let's Eat!

When I was growing up, moms cooked the food. That was pretty much the only option, and in my fairly homogenized suburban existence, I didn't know any kids without a mom. My dad certainly never cooked, with two exceptions, which occurred when Mom was gone at mealtime. This happened maybe three times throughout my childhood. Where did Mom go? What was she doing? She had no driver's license. Had she set out on foot around five o'clock some evening? The answers are lost in the clouds of history. But Mom's disappearance meant one thing. It meant fried bologna.

As the name hints, fried bologna consists of taking the lunch meat—*which was supposed to be for lunch!*—and frying it. Only Dad could do this because it was clearly dangerous and more than a little crazy. Bologna for dinner? What next? Tinfoil hats and alien landings on the lawn? As it turned out, no. Fried bologna is simply the common sandwich staple with little cuts in it so it wouldn't curl up in the skillet. You heat it up, and it's…a warm bologna sandwich. We never missed Mom more.

To make up for the "meh" that was fried bologna, dessert was Marshmallow Surprise. Don't for a minute think dessert was automatic. Vegetables were automatic. A slice of bread was automatic. Milk? Automatic. But dessert was a rarity. So Marshmallow Surprise was a pretty big deal. The way it's made can, maybe for the first time, be made public here:

## Marshmallow Surprise

*1 cookie sheet*
*Crackers (saltines, preferably)*
*Big marshmallows, the kind that make you want s'more*

Lay the crackers on the cookie sheet. Lay the marshmallows on the crackers. Put the cookie sheet in the oven. (Only Dad can touch the oven, so no details on settings. Um, hot?) Cook until marshmallows are golden brown. Remove and eat.

Celebrate the fact that, while Mom has mysteriously disappeared, this wondrous treat has arrived.

It was marshmallows slightly melted on crackers, so why was it called a surprise? You could look through the tinted window in the oven door and literally watch the magic happen. It was all kinds of good, but no kind of surprise. I think Dad named it, and, while he was a good pastor, he was not gifted in the area of marketing.

That was my culinary base. Mom did something in the kitchen while I watched TV. Dad did the thing with bologna. When it was time to feed myself, I broke new ground, but I didn't dig very deep. At all.

During the summers of my later teen years, my brother and sister and I were on our own for many summer days. Mom and Dad were both at work, Dad's fairly flexible ministry schedule making him available for enough unexpected drop-ins that we never got up to anything unsavory.

My sister, DeeAnn, was still six years younger than I, and still mostly just an irritant. She would eventually grow into one of my absolute favorite people, one of the best writers I've ever known, and a lifelong friend—for a life that wasn't nearly long enough. But what she ate in the summer when I was 16 was really none of my concern. My brother, Damon, and I were working men. We had grocery store jobs, and we got hungry. Here's how we assuaged that.

We would buy blueberry muffin mix. The brand was important, but so as not to hurt the feelings of any of the other fine brands available, let's just say you could make this one quickly. In a jiffy, even. Butter, egg, powdery deliciousness, 12 to 15 minutes in the oven, and you're good to go. One guy slices, the other guy chooses. Still the best way to make sure the muffin split is fair.

You've had your half box of muffins. Now what do you want? A half gallon of chocolate ice cream, that's what. Again, one guy makes the cut, the other guy scoops his half out of the box. A system that is perfect in its beauty. This was our summertime staple, and you can see that it covers the two most important food groups: a warm bread thing and a cold thing. Sometimes we'd get fancy and go for chocolate marshmallow ice cream instead of regular chocolate just to keep it interesting. Oh, and an important caveat: These treats are best enjoyed while watching TV.

More than 40 years later, I still have no idea how to bake anything. At all. My go-to when I'm feeding myself is a chicken breast heated up on a grill named after a heavyweight boxer, cut up and put in a bowl of lentils that have spent exactly one minute in a microwave. Makes me kind of hungry just thinking about it.

# 53

# Christian Youth Theater

When you get married young, and you haven't even known each other for even a year, there are a lot of things you don't know about each other.

For example, I had no idea my wife was interested in children's youth theater. Also, my wife did not know she was interested in children's youth theater. Turns out that she was. She really, really was, and still is.

A few years after we moved to Kansas, my parents semiretired and moved here as well. Preachers never really retire beyond "semi," and my dad preached in one way or another for the rest of his life. Eventually, my brother and sister moved to the middle of the country as well. When they did, my brother's kids missed being in CYT.

CYT stands for Christian Youth Theater. It's a big organization that started in San Diego and now has branches all over the country.

Kids perform musicals, parents do all the work, and at the end of each show, people applaud the kids. Good system, right? I forgot to mention that parents also pay for everything, but we get no applause for that.

My wife and sister-in-law started and ran the Kansas City branch of CYT for a long time. Seemed long to me, anyway. I am not Show People.

Are you Show People? You can find out by answering a few quick questions:

- Do you know what a ball change is? Hint: If you think it's a way to make the toilet stop running, then you are not Show People.

- Do you know that *Les Miserables* isn't just an old book about how to get free bread?

- Do you know the green room is never actually green—and sometimes it's not a room at all, but just an area?

- Do you know that you can be weirdly moved by children singing about the French Revolution?

If you're looking at four "nos," then you are not Show People. I wasn't either. I'm still not, but I know a lot more about it than I used to.

For example, my kids have been:

- Joseph's musical brothers

- Annie's orphan pals

- Questionable employees of a bar in the French Revolution (not as disturbing as it sounds, but kind of disturbing)

- One of seven brides and one of seven brothers

- Native Americans winning over John Smith

- Munchkins

- Tom Sawyer's fence painters

- Lots and lots of other things, most of which involved glitter in some form

If you're not Show People, you might not know that glitter is the most insidious of all craft supplies. I have stood, shakily, on a four-section-high scaffold above a stage adjusting lights and climbed down to find glitter in my hair. It. Gets. *Everywhere*.

The musical version of glitter is the songs that constitute the performances. They get into your head in a way that nothing else can. Math formulas? Bible verses? Internet passwords? They are nothing compared to a song about whether you can hear the people singing or not. Spoiler alert: You can. You really can, and you can't stop.

My wife has directed shows, which means she's done every job from top to bottom. I've done only what you'd call the bottom jobs.

I wasn't the lighting guy. I was the guy who put the wrong color of plastic film over the light and had to change it six times.

I wasn't the musical director. I was the guy who crawled under the stage to find where to plug in the speakers.

I wasn't the set designer or the set constructor. I was the guy who carried in the boards and then carried out the boards once the show was over.

I wasn't the prop manager. I was the guy who tripped over the props because I was in the wrong place at the wrong time, in the dark.

I wasn't in charge of the green room. I was in charge of vacuuming the green room, which, while sometimes not a room, always has a floor.

CYT was an amazing time for both of our kids, and I'm endlessly grateful that they got to do it. We still support this organization, but in ways that involve a lot less scaffold climbing and a lot less of our time.

. . . . . . . . . . . . .

This may come as a shock to you, but your kids might not want to do the things you did when you were young. Maybe you played football. Maybe you were a Girl Scout. Maybe you just helped your parents work on the farm. Chances are good that you have kids who don't want to do *any* of that.

Over and over again, I saw parents' faces glow while they watched their very average kid singing in a group of very average kids who had come together to make something very above average. And more times than I can count, I heard parents say, "We did not know how to relate to our kid because he or she didn't want to play football or be in scouts or work on the farm. But this, portraying a lamp who turns into a person at the end of a musical about a monster and a girl who likes to read? This is how we relate to our kid."

You see that happen, and you know what it does to you? It almost makes you Show People.

## 54

# Putting the "Nuclear" in Nuclear Family

For lots of people over the years, the idea of a vacation meant getting into a car that held the whole family and driving as far as possible. Sometimes that was the whole thing, just the drive. Get there, turn around, and drive back. The destination could be anything—an amusement park, Grandma's house, or a giant ball of something.

The idea of the road trip holds a certain romance I totally get. Eating pork rinds and getting semi drivers to honk their horns and seeing license plates from *not* your state? Who doesn't love that?

Me. I don't love that. I love the idea, and now, through the magic of podcasts and blue teeth and whatnot, you can be thoroughly entertained for the duration of your trip to Durango or wherever. But here's the thing: Driving makes me mad. Not mildly irritated. More like a Hulk without the muscles or the green skin or the lucrative multiple-movie deal.

Specifically, it's not *my* driving that makes me mad. I don't mind that. With enough coffee and enough bathrooms, I could drive forever. It's the other drivers who get to me. Too fast, too slow, too many lane changes, not enough lane changes. That thing where they drive down the lane that everybody knows is about to close—all of it irritates me.

My wife, on the other hand, harbors none of these driving demons. She cruises down the highway with a song in her heart and compassion and warmth for every type of driver.

Except me. She gets mad at me for getting mad. Then I get mad at her for getting mad at me, but I also get mad at myself for getting mad. So I'm triple-mad now, and we can still see our house in the rearview mirror.

So why would we go on a 774-mile road trip with our two adult-sized children? Well, partly because they were not just adult-sized. They were actual adults. One of them would soon be married. This was to be our last trip as a nuclear family, and we had seen others do it. People who did not seem to possess any superpowers or great spiritual depth have driven back and forth across America like a walk in the park. But it was a drive in a car.

Thus, we were determined that we could hit the road without hitting the roof. We were going to will ourselves to avoid being…ourselves.

It did not work. The first part, the part where we left Kansas and headed west, went fine. There was not much to bump into between Kansas and Colorado, where we eventually started seeing mountains. We just drove along, looking out the window at nothing. The first day went by without a problem.

Then we hit construction. Why? No one knows. The roads are always being repaired, but the roads never *are* repaired. There are monks who spend a lifetime pondering this very question, but they find no answer. The construction closed the one road we needed to traverse. Now our map did us no good. Our app did us no good. Neither did driving underneath crows so we could go where they were going.

Then a guy in a yellow plastic hat waved us onto a dirt path. We had to go where he waved us. It was peer pressure. If we leave the beaten path, then it's anarchy. There is no longer a rule of law. The constitution is thrown out the window. It's every traveler for him- or herself.

Obviously, Lana and I turned on each other at this point. But we tried to do it in a way the kids couldn't witness and record. After all, one of them was about to get married! We didn't want to undo a couple of decades of stellar molding and modeling in a few literal (and figurative) bumpy miles! There might be some happy young couples who say, "We always try to do whatever our parents did *not* do." We didn't want to be those kinds of parents.

Unfortunately, an under-the-radar fight is still a fight. Oh, not the shouting and throwing things kind of fight. We never do that. With us, it's more of the gritted-teeth smiling and saying things that, if read, don't sound bad, but if heard sound very bad indeed. My wife knows how to say, "Whatever you want, honey" in a way that I know means the exact opposite. I can respond with, "Excellent, great!" in a way we both know connotes neither excellence nor greatness.

This went on for about 400 miles. But at least there was lots of dust. And sizable rocks.

We eventually got to Colorado and had a great time. We hiked enough in the beautiful mountains to determine that none of us really like hiking in beautiful mountains. We whitewater-rafted on a river so serene that the guide kept apologizing. But we kept saying, "No, really, this is just what we needed."

We rode a train that someone else was driving, so that was perfect. It was a time I'm going to remember fondly for as long as I remember things, except for one little part.

The place we were staying was a place where you have to share time. Some friends loaned it to us, and it was terrific. Great accommodations, convenient location. And, as we checked in, we were handed a 50-dollar gift certificate to a local restaurant. Yay! All we had to do was sit through a three-hour presentation about time and how you share it. We got to cut an hour off by promising that we had just borrowed the place and were never, ever going to share time. Ever. The people in charge took that news well, considering, but they still made us sit through an impressive presentation about how dumb we were for not taking them up on the deal of a lifetime.

The local restaurant was nice, and after a fun week of shared time, we prepared to head home.

We steeled ourselves to really, really get along and to be really, really calm and kind, especially to each other.

This did not work at all. Eventually, Lana and I let the kids in on the fact that we were kind of fighting. They said, "We kind of know." Then we talked about conflict in an open and honest way—which I am sure did very little good.

There won't be another vacation like that one, ever. There are grand-babies now, and there are "others" who are significant. Our family hasn't just gotten bigger. It's gotten better. When our two grandchildren came along, our capacity to love new people grew to new heights. We couldn't be happier with our family. But we will never drive 774 miles with them either.

And that's why there won't be another vacation like that one. Ever.

# 55

# This Mission Is a Trip: Mexico Edition

A lot of thought has gone into the idea of mission trips. Especially the kind of trips that take privileged kids from comfortable places and put them into direct contact with unprivileged kids in uncomfortable places.

I've helped sponsor two trips to the not-vacation, not-beach part of Mexico. I've also been to the not-Bourbon Street part of New Orleans twice, and I've learned a lot.

For example, I've learned that there are only two places I ever want to sleep: my own bed (choice number 1) and a hotel (usually distant choice number 2—unless a *this-is-a-moral-issue* amount of money has been spent, and the price includes someone making me an omelet in the morning).

The things I remember about Mexico, just like everything else that I remember, come to me in flashes. Are these flash memories accurate? Let's assume not. Did they even actually happen? Probably, mostly. Anyway, here they are.

Crossing the border into Mexico is a very serious thing, and you have to make your passenger van full of kids be very quiet. A good way to do this is to scare them with the idea of prison in a foreign country and how they'll certainly end up there if they make a sound while I talk to the nice man in the uniform. Using some of the same techniques I perfected taking a school bus of rowdy kids up a mountain, I got my missions kids to sit very still and contemplate the cost of failure. Worked like a charm.

It was fun to see suburban kids working! They were wresting wheelbarrows, placing pavers, painting, planting, hauling—it just warms the heart.

When it comes to spiritual lessons, you can get deeper on a mission trip than you can at camp. When you're teaching kids who have worked an honest half day or so and they're exhausted and a little disoriented, they listen better than they do when their entire focus is who they're going to sit by at campfire.

We slept in a tentlike building—canvas stretched over a curved metal framework—with a dirt floor. When it rained, the rain poured across the ground and covered almost everything with mud.

Bugs really liked the rain, and if you thought there were already a lot of them in the canvas structure thing, surprise! Many billions more were on the way. Pro tip: Sleep in the van you came in, with a shirt wrapped around your head to keep the bugs out of your ears. How did the bugs get into the van? Unknowable. But there were a few billion fewer bugs in the van than there were in the Hogan. So that was nice.

The food was good, and there was a lot of it—but nothing so photogenic that you'd be compelled to take a picture and post it on social media.

The local kids were universally adorable. So much so that you had to keep reminding yourself that you were really looking at abject poverty. Many of the kids we saw were living in what was technically an orphanage, but they were not orphans. Their parents just knew they were so much better off at the orphanage, so that's where they dropped them. They would come to visit occasionally. To visit *their own children*. It wasn't easy to explain this kind of poverty to our kids. I did not understand it myself.

The guy who ran one of the orphanages was really scary. Not to the kids—the kids loved him. He was so invested in his mission that he intimidated us relatively wealthy adults. For example, he told us one story of a donor who offered to donate his old van because he was going to buy a new one. The guy responded, "Why don't you donate the new van?" The idea being, "Give God your best, not your discards!"

See? Scary.

On the other Mexico trip, we served at various work sites. As we approached a church where we were going to install a drop ceiling, I noticed a pile of scrap lumber. It looked like a small pile of pallet parts, along with some tree branches and a piece of tarp. Then a guy climbed out from under it. Then another guy. They lived there, in that hazardous pile of nothing.

On that same trip, we were mixing concrete for the foundation of a new building on the edge of what passed for a town. Locals would come out and bring us some of the best food I've ever eaten. One day a man came and insisted on helping, even though he appeared to be pretty old. He carted the wheelbarrow full of wet concrete back and forth from where it was being mixed, and he wouldn't accept any help. He worked tirelessly all day. As he was leaving, I spoke to him for a minute, utilizing my three years of B-minus-level of Spanish from high school. He was full of gratitude. He couldn't thank us enough. I learned later that he was 80.

Both Mexico mission trips were capped off by a stop in Texas, where we visited the biggest water park I've ever seen. We spent the day splishing and splashing and plummeting down steep curvy slides and floating along on something called a lazy river. I hoped this diversion wouldn't undermine all we had done and seen. I hoped that the irony would not be lost on any of my mission kids: One day out from witnessing the most profound need we would ever experience up-close, we were lounging in a place where even the river was lazy.

# 56

# This Mission Is a Trip:
# New Orleans Edition

Prior to my mission trip to New Orleans, I had been there only once, on a business trip 20 years prior.

Then Hurricane Katrina hit, and Christians got interested. Before that, we mainly thought of New Orleans as a place with a lot of bars and wrought iron. And bars made of wrought iron, now that I think about it. It was not a place you visit with your men's Wednesday morning Bible study group. But I'm proud (not in the sinful pride way, of course) to say that people of faith swarmed into the Ninth Ward, and, while we didn't fix everything, we fixed some things. That's better than no things.

When you're going to help rebuild a place that's been flooded, where houses have been razed to their foundations, here's another pro tip: Learn to tape drywall first.

Knowing a trade, even one you had not professionally plied in a quarter century, meant you got to do something you already knew how to do. This is much better than the alternative. I got to tape seams in houses and help restore places so people could live in them again. It was a blessing and an honor.

My wife, a jack of no trades, was also blessed and honored. She had to scrape mold off of two-by-fours and then spray them with "let's not have any more mold" spray. Sure, this sounds like a fun job, and at first it probably is. Around day four, however, the thrill dissipates. Or so I'm told. I was having a great nostalgic time doing something most home-owners avoid like…mold. And here's the benefit of volunteer work: Even if you're merely mediocre at what you're doing, everyone involved appreciates your effort. If you're actually good, that's gravy.

Speaking of gravy, we ate really well in New Orleans. People made us food, and, remember, this is a place where tourists go *for the food*. That's key. No one goes to Indiana for the food. There might be some fine cooks there, but I'm pretty sure no one has ever had a great meal, leaned back, unbuckled his straining belt, and sighed, "Ah! Just like in Indiana!"

It's hard to find something to do that makes you feel better than rebuilding someone's house. You get a deep sense of validation, an idea that you've found God's will for that time, and He put you in that place for a reason.

Then you start to wonder why He didn't provide better bedding.

On one trip to New Orleans, we slept in church. Yes, it's something that millions do every single Sunday, but when you do it at night, and you've been doing labor that is 100 percent more physical than usual, you do not want to sleep in church. Specifically, a few people slept on inflatable mattresses, while most of us stretched out on pews or on the floor. There are a lot of great things that happen in churches worldwide. Getting a good night's sleep isn't one of them.

On the other trip, we slept in FEMA trailers. Each trailer had two or three compartments that held bunk beds and a bathroom. They resembled tiny, portable dorms, and they weren't bad, except for one design feature. The walls that separated you from the next room were only about 7 feet high. Above that was open space. The entire trailer, end to end, was open at the top. I suppose this was to promote air circulation and stuff like that. This meant that, while you had visual separation, you were pretty much all staying in one big room. Everyone heard every conversation, every snore, and every other noise, whatever it might be. Fortunately, we were all too tired to notice. Much.

And speaking of sleeping, we stayed overnight in Memphis on the way home. Memphis is a super cool city. You should go. Across the street from Elvis's old house, there's a hotel that has a pool shaped like a guitar. If that alone does not have you packing your bags, let me quickly add that the hotel has one of those little griddles where you can make your own waffles. We were finishing up our delicious waffle breakfast when a woman came in and set up a life-sized, die-cut Elvis.

I assume that most everyone in Memphis has one of these in their car. This woman was certainly proud of her Elvis. She set up a small table and placed copies of a book on it—a book she had written about her affair with Elvis. This was an exercise, as you might guess, in politely avoiding eye contact and trying to act as if you had something pressing that was about to begin somewhere else.

Fortunately, some of the other hotel guests were on their way to Graceland, so getting to meet a woman with a connection to the King was a highlight of their trip. As they lined up to buy books and get autographs, we were able to grab a couple more waffles and head home.

# 57

# DDIY (Don't Do It Yourself)

Some people see a problem and ask, "How can I fix this?" Other people see a problem and ask, "Who can I call to fix this?" I am other people.

About 40 years ago, I learned how to tape drywall seams. Since then, I have not learned any new skills. In fact, I have forgotten some of what I once knew. I once started socking money away so I could buy a new lawnmower rather than trying to change the blade on my old one.

Every picture or mirror or other heavy thing I've hung on a wall was preceded by a trail of nail-sized holes I used to find the stud. And the sad part is that I know where the studs are.

"Sixteen on center," as the term suggests, means that the middle of each stud is 16 inches from the previous one. So, you start in a corner. There should be a stud about a foot and a half away. Sometimes, though, there just isn't. You learn this by pounding a nail that's going in way too easily, a nail that's meant to hold your semi-valuable decor from a mid-range decor store. If you can't find a stud even though you've clearly put sixteen inches' worth of holes in the wall, you have to install a molly. Mollies are plastic things that don't work. Have I made hanging a picture sound like way too big a deal? No, no. I have not. Have I spent hundreds of dollars over the years on stud finders? I think you know the answer.

I've also failed at plumbing and electrical work, enough so that I plan to never again do any plumbing or electrical work. You plumb wrong; you flood your home. You electric wrong; you die. There's just too much at stake.

Landscaping is also off the table. A couple of years ago, I tried to install a French drain in my backyard. What makes it French? No idea. I bet it's like fries. If you go to actual France, they don't call them that. Then they make fun of you for ordering them.

Installing the French drain is really simple—if you do it the way that doesn't work. You take a plastic pipe and lay it where the water is already running every time it rains. Then you put rocks around the pipe to hide the fact that it's not going to work. Now all you have to do is wait for the next big rain. Then you get a cup of coffee and sit looking out the window while the drain does nothing and the water runs faster because of the rocks. It's a dramatic look, and if you just tell people that you and God have worked together to add a water feature to your yard, that almost makes sense.

Can you fail at just putting down pavers? Yup. There are maybe three steps you need to follow to get the flat pieces of concrete to just lie there, flatly. That's too many steps for me. I'm good for one step, poorly done, and maybe half of another step. In other words, I kind of dig around in the dirt a bit, then lay the paver down. Then I jump on the paver till it seems pretty level. Repeat. My advice? Call a landscaping company or invest in mulch.

Mulch is the universal symbol of defeat. It's a white flag that comes in more natural colors. If it were cul-de-sac acceptable, our whole yard would be mulch. A thick bed of mulch over weed-inhibitor fabric. Weed-inhibitor fabric, as you have no doubt already surmised, is the fabric you put down first if you don't want weeds to grow up through your mulch. In New Mexico, some people just throw in the towel and replace their yards with concrete that they paint green. There's a word for these people. Geniuses.

The internet has made it possible to quickly and easily watch lots of people do simple homeowner projects I will never do. In other words, there's some kind of conspiracy wherein professionals pose as regular people and make it look like anybody can do things that nobody can do. It's as if Cirque Du Soleil performers put on an old pair of Dockers and a T-shirt. They do an entire act and then look right into the camera and say, "It's easy!"

Chopping down a tree is a good example of this phenomenon. There are thousands, if not hundreds, of videos showing everyone from octogenarians to precocious children chopping down sequoias. Not with chainsaws, either, as much as I wanted to buy a giant chainsaw. No, the people in the videos use good old axes.

So when the willow in the backyard got some kind of willow disease, I got an ax. I watched the videos, and away I went.

About halfway through, I thought of gloves. The gloves went on easily over my blisters and held in the blood, so that was handy.

In the videos, the ax bit deeply and cleanly into the wood. I mostly tried not to hit the tree with the flat part.

The wounded willow trunk had about the same girth as a mason jar. An eight-year-old in a video I watched cut down a similar tree in about ten whacks. After half an hour, I had put a pretty good dent in the bark.

Daunted, I turned to plan B, for which there was no internet video. Plan B consisted of throwing a rope around the highest part of the tree. This, like everything else, apparently, is harder to do than it looks. I tied a useless French drain rock around a rope and threw it. About a dozen times. Finally, the rope wrapped around a branch that was strong enough and high enough to make a difference. Then I got my wife to hold on to the end of the rope and pull.

Nothing happened. Nothing at all. So I chopped a few more chops and joined Lana in pulling on the rope. The tree didn't budge. This chop and pull trade-off went on for another half hour or so. Finally, we heard the sweetest sound (next to a baby's first cry or slot machine signaling a big win): a tiny cracking noise.

Affirmed, encouraged, and motivated, we accelerated the chop/pull cycle. Soon the tree was gracefully swooping toward the house, so we pulled the rope sideways and most of the tree came down. A year or so later, the two-foot-high stump rotted enough so that I could pull it out with one hand.

This small win did a lot for me on the inside. It taught me that if I really apply myself, if I *really* put my mind and body into it…I should call someone even sooner in the process.

# 58

# Table for Four

Some people collect baseball cards. Some collect stamps. Some people collect autographs, and others collect comic books. What do these collectibles have in common? Their intrinsic value isn't a lot. A stamp is worth a stamp, as far as the USPS is concerned. And a comic book isn't worth much at all if you don't "get it," which I don't.

However, when any of these items is rare, it can be worth much more than its ink and paper.

This same principle can apply to people. For example, if you are part of a couple, and you have "couple friends," then you know they are worth more than all of the rare stamps and autographed baseball cards in the world.

My wife and I have figured out the things we like to do together, and we make space for the things we *don't* want to do together. For example, she can go to see all the musicals she wants. I can go to all the action movies. Together we watch TV shows about people getting a new backsplash. It's a great system.

But it took years of compromise and discussion to land here. Early in our marriage, I watched a lot of people sing about what they hoped the next 90 minutes of music might bring them, while my wife had to witness more than her share of big-screen car chases.

Finding another couple who have reached this level and can mix and match with you? That is like finding a unicorn with an *Amazing Spider-Man* issue volume 1, which I am assuming would be very rare.

You might like the husband and only be so-so on the wife. Or the wife might be great, but the husband makes you feel as if you have to run an emotional obstacle course every time you're together. Sometimes the husband is easygoing, but the wife makes eggshells look easy to walk on. Other times, the wife is the salt of the earth, and the husband is just salty.

If you're looking for a couple to be couple friends with, you might think your job is a good place to start. It just isn't.

Yes, you have lots in common with your coworkers. The "co" prefix should be a pretty good hint. You have challenges, successes, shared jokes, and a bright future in whatever industry you're toiling in together. Your spouse does not have those challenges, successes, shared jokes, or bright future. This doesn't matter at all—unless you're at a restaurant and you've just heard the specials described, and you realize that you have an hour or so ahead of you and need to discover some common conversational horizons.

My wife's coworkers are some of the nicest people who have ever lived. She's a school nurse, so her peers are people who are in charge of the future. I don't think there's a more important job, but I don't really want to spend an evening hearing two people talk about nursing in detail while a hapless spouse and I try to look interested.

My coworkers are some of the funniest people who've ever lived. But believe me, no one wants to be "on" for a few hours with someone who's that funny. It's exhausting. And the details of the greeting card job are just like the details of any other job. They're interesting only to the people doing the job.

Your church can be a good place to look for couple friends. People generally talk less about work there, and it's typical for couples to drive there together, sit together, and leave together. Some churches try to get couples to make friends via "small group" programs. This *kind of* works— in the way people say that when they really mean, "It doesn't work at all."

You can't have friends assigned to you by a very well-meaning associate pastor who has all the couples' names on a magnetic board in his or her office. We were part of a culling process once, in which group members were chosen by their availability on a specific night. That's just too wide a net.

But let's say you've found a promising couple, and you want to give the couple-friendship a try. Now you need to find something of mutual interest. This is where you find out that lots of couples have interests you do not find interesting.

We know couples who golf. Neither of us has ever swung a club. We know couples who play bridge. Neither of us has ever swung whatever you swing when you're playing bridge. We know couples who love to go to the lake or soccer games or casinos or museums. All those things seem fine, but I really don't want to do any of them. So you see the problem.

Turns out that there's a long list of things I can pretend to enjoy doing, and a very short list of things I actually enjoy doing. It's much easier to convince my wife she's having fun, but that just highlights the difficulty. That's her pet name for me, by the way: The Difficulty.

We are very fortunate to have found a few people in a few places over the years we could be couple-friends with. Some of the best times I've ever had have been in their company. I'm not going to tell you anything else about them. They belong to us. You cannot have them.

Maybe you can find your own couple friends and try golf. I hear it's awesome.

# 59

# Use Your Legs, Not Your Back

When I started high school, there was no such thing as computers. Well, there were a few computers. They were in Houston, and you used them if you had a problem. In space.

But at the start of my junior year, our high school got a computer and started using it to schedule the 400 or so students in various classes. And that's how 400 or so students ended up in one gym class. It looked like the best-attended pep rally in the history of pep, but it was just one class. For everyone.

So the kids were divvied up, and to make it all work out, there was a thing called zero hour PE. The down side of zero hour PE was that it happened before school started, somewhere around seven o'clock. That was also the upside. Sometimes the coaches forgot the class even existed.

I'd drive up to the school. No coach would be there. I'd drive away. Good system! One time, I showed up at the same time as a few other students. No coaches in sight. So we headed to McDonald's, where they had recently begun experiments with eggs and muffins. The coach pulled into the parking lot as we exited. We pretended we didn't see him waving and shouting at us.

On the rare days that the coaches did show up to unlock the doors and turn on the lights, they would then retreat to their offices and read the newspaper. This was our cue to take a nap on the wrestling mats. This was a great educational system. Everyone got good grades, because you started out with extra credit by being one of the true American heroes who volunteered for zero hour PE.

That's the kind of exercise ethic that I carried into adulthood and still employ today. This is no idle boast. I have a body that demonstrates years of barely doing anything—and doing it only in the most halfhearted way.

More like quarterhearted, or an even smaller fraction. (I also never cared about math, so I can't be any more precise than that.)

My brother and I had the obligatory My First Hernia™ weight and bench set that went all the way up to 135 pounds or so. We incorrectly did very little on it as well.

As an adult, I've gone to the gym like most people, mainly, so I can say, "I've been to the gym." Back when it was trendy, I went to aerobics class and paced myself to do slightly better than whoever was oldest. This is all background information for what happened one night when my daughter, Paige, came home from college.

. . . . . . . . . . . .

She went to her room in the basement. Before you assume we're cruel people, you should know that the basement is finished and is indistinguishable from the rest of the house, except that it's under the house. The room was, in fact, very nice. She wasn't down there like a Harriet Potter or something. At any rate, my wife and I were out, and my daughter called us to ask if we were aware that her ceiling was leaking. We were not. But it was.

Some CSI-level sleuthing helped us realize that the refrigerator was leaking through the floor, then through the mysterious space between floors. Water ended up dripping from the basement ceiling. We figured this out by moving the fridge into the garage and waiting to see what happened next.

We got the refrigerator fixed. It had a broken something-underneath-it. With a new one in place, it stopped leaking. But now it had to be moved from the garage and back into the kitchen.

To accomplish this, I enlisted my wife, my son, and my daughter. Why not a couple of neighbors, you ask? Good question! Here's the bad answer: There's something about the suburban guy mind that balks at the idea of asking for help. With anything, but certainly not with something you can imagine your neighbor doing on his own. Is this dumb? Does it smack of a dumb kind of pride? Oh, yeah. It really does, but I can't begin to count all the things I've tried to do myself instead of asking for help. Not contractor stuff—that's what hiring people is for. I mean moving furniture or putting a ladder on a table instead of borrowing a taller one for the job. That kind of thing.

So the fridge is coming out the garage door, through the front door, and back into the kitchen. To do this, it has to go up one step. Just one, a little landing by the front door. We stalled at this juncture and decided to hold a family conference.

At this point in my life, I had moved hundreds of refrigerators. Somehow, I got on the list of go-to guys for moving from one house to another, both at church and at work. I did it a bunch. In fact, I occasionally helped a friend who had an actual moving business. None of that would matter here.

My idea was to lean the fridge toward my wife and daughter, the two family members with the least upper-body strength. My son and I would take the majority of the 300 or so pounds up the step, and there you go. I got outvoted on this. How did this task become a democracy? No idea. But the thinking among the majority was that the fridge could be scratched by the concrete step, so it ought to, instead, be lifted straight up into the air (six inches or so) and then moved into the house. Each of the four of us gets a corner, and up it goes. Democracy at work.

"On three. Ready? One, two, three..."

I lifted my part. And everyone else's part. My wife, my son, and my daughter, in a separate meeting had apparently colluded to *not* go on three. Were they waiting for four? I never found out because I was distracted by what was happening to my right arm. There was a popping sound and then, like a window shade being rolled up, I watched my bicep change. Specifically, the tendons holding it stopped holding it, possibly recognizing that they were no match for an entire refrigerator. The muscle, unrestricted by the lower tendon, kind of bunched up and looked like it was flexing, which it wasn't. I think I yelled. It's all kind of a blur. We got the fridge back into the kitchen. The next day I went to the doctor, although I hoped that maybe my arm would work itself out.

This is not the kind of thing that works itself out. The doctor said he recommended surgery for anyone under 50. I was never so glad to be over 50.

Today, you can tell something is wrong with my arm if you look closely. But it's no big deal. As I mentioned, I wasn't really lifting weights a lot anyway.

Next time, I'll hire somebody to move the refrigerator.

# 60

# Not-So-Tiny Dancer

In the 1960s and 1970s, the kids in our faith tradition went to public school. There was no such thing as homeschooling, at least where we lived. And private school was only in movies or maybe for really rich people from the East Coast or something.

Public school presented no theological conflicts for anyone. Most of my classmates went to church somewhere, even if Dad stayed home and watched football pregame shows on TV instead. And schools didn't teach anything that churches were against, so there was no controversy, at least that I knew about.

The exception was dancing. In gym class. With girls.

You could get out of gym-dancing for religious reasons if your parents sent a note. Dancing was like sex education—that very vague class in which a male coach confused the boys while the female school nurse said nothing specific or helpful to the girls. A few kids got "noted" out of sex ed, but nobody skipped dancing.

There was no real reason to avoid it, even for the most conservative student. In the early 1970s, I was in seventh grade, and boys and girls were still petrified of each other, for the most part. We had to be encouraged to hold each other *closer* while dancing, not warned against the opposite.

We learned some dances we would never do outside of gym class. There was one where you made a box shape over and over with your feet. It was supposed to approximate a waltz. It very well might have. I had exactly zero chances to waltz again, ever, so I don't know.

The other dance I remember was the Virginia Reel. Really.

This antebellum relic was probably first enjoyed in the ballrooms of plantation homes. It involved standing in lines and clapping your hands.

Then, couples would go into a disputed space between the lines, link arms at the elbow, and spin. Clearly, there was plenty of "room for the Holy Spirit" during the Virginia Reel. In fact, it was a dance that acted as birth control. It combined the most awkward elements of gym class and sex ed. Trust me: Nobody was thinking about sex while dizzily spinning between two lines of clapping classmates.

The waltz had a more brutal pairing system. Boys lined up on one side of the gym, girls on the other. When a coach blew a whistle, boys would run to the girl they wanted to make infinity boxes with. Or, in fairness, sometimes the girls would get to run to their chosen boys.

Fortunately, I had a girl who was a friend (a very technical and oft-explained distinction in seventh grade). Through a series of furtive nods and gestures, we determined we would run to each other every time. I don't remember her name or what she looked like, but she saved me thousands of dollars in therapy. I hope I did the same for her.

Coincidentally, a series of furtive nods and gestures would become my go-to move. It worked okay throughout high school and right up until I used it successfully on my wife.

Dancing remained a theological gray area for our church since that sweaty middle school introduction. It was never technically forbidden, as it was by some churches. Was this because 2 Samuel 6:14 says that King David "danced before the Lord"? Maybe. But no one said you couldn't, and our church never held a counterprogramming event like Anti-Prom, as some churches did.

But we never really encouraged dancing either. There was no dancing at weddings in our church, for example. We knew there had to be dancing somewhere. We heard rumors that there was dancing at Polish weddings. We heard about a thing called a Chicken Dance, which sounded silly and fun, but it wasn't for us.

As a Bible college student, I was not allowed to enter a bar. Not for a Diet Coke. Not for a caffeine-free Diet Coke, even. If you can't go where somebody's drinking, you probably don't have to worry about dancing.

Now and then I would end up at an off-brand wedding and hop

around a little bit, or sway, making boxes, as I had been taught. Strangely, the Virginia Reel never came up.

Today, the rules have loosened some. I got to dance with my just-married daughter at her wedding reception, and I wouldn't trade that for anything.

# 61

# Dance Like You Have Insurance

Over the years, the loosened-up dancing rules have become so loose that a church friend of ours actually hosted a party where there was intentional, deliberate dancing. First, there was live music, supplied by the guys from our Sunday morning worship team, so that was fun. It made us feel cooler than we were used to feeling.

Then, because technology was making all kinds of things possible, someone started playing music you could dance to. Soon, people started dancing. Noticing that the first dancing couple was not struck by lightning, others joined in.

The lightning was a real possibility because this was an indoor/outdoor kind of party, held in a barn. Not a farm barn, but not a town barn either. It was a kind of straddle-barn that connected the two. Inside the barn were tables laden with catered food, warming in those big aluminum pans that make it look as if you could eat for days. Outside the barn was a concrete pad about the size of a standard driveway. That was the dance floor.

For a while, it was fun to dance. I'm not very good at dancing, but I'm very dedicated. My philosophy: If you look like you mean it, people will be less likely to question it. This is actually my philosophy for several things besides dancing.

My wife and I were somewhat rhythmically hopping around when a song I really like came on. It's from the early 1980s. It details what I like about you. In fact, they say that over and over. Then they yell, "Hey!"

If you have a heart, if you have a soul, if you understand what life and love and music are all about, then you jump up and down when they say "Hey!" You jump as high as you can, straight up, and by the time you hit the ground, you are already on your way back up.

Then you feel a snapping sensation in your foot. Then you keep jumping. Then the song ends, and you tell your wife that maybe it's time to go home. You might have broken something.

Here's the weird part: My brother, two years younger than I, was at this same party. Musically speaking, we're from the same era, and he has a heart and a soul and all that other stuff. So he was jumping too. And when the song ended, he also knew something was wrong with *his* foot.

We left that barn, two couples. We walked up the long gravel drive to our cars. We were leaning on our wives. We looked a lot like that famous painting of the soldiers barely surviving the Revolutionary War. Here's what our wives did—the women who had pledged "in sickness and health." They laughed all the way up that long drive. They thought it was hilarious that their husbands were so old now that they could get injured while dancing.

It was slightly less hilarious the next day when the X-rays came back and revealed that my brother and I had both broken bones in our feet. Specifically, the same bone (one in his foot, one in mine).

There's nothing to be done for a hairline fracture of a bone on the outer edge of your foot. You get a Frankenstein boot and try to stay off it as much as possible.

I clomped around for the appointed amount of time. It wasn't too bad. My chair at work has wheels on it, and I could get most places just rollin' with it. There's a kind of dramatic impact when you enter a staff meeting pushing your chair with one good leg and dragging a giant plastic boot on the other. People got me coffee. I didn't have to mow the grass. It took several weeks and eventually got almost totally healed.

My foot still hurts sometimes when the weather changes, just like all old people have said about pains forever. And it hurts now and then if I walk too far—or just randomly to remind me what happens when old people dance. Sometimes I dance anyway, but the times are getting further and further apart. Each time I dance, I think, *This is probably the last time.*

One of these days, I'll be right.

# 62

# I Wrote (Half of) a Musical

About a year after I came to Hallmark, we started making something called Shoebox Cards. We still make them, and it's still one of my favorite parts of the job. But back then, it was pretty much all I did.

At first, it was just birthday cards. Then we added seasonal cards—Mother's Day, Christmas, Halloween. Then we added non-card kinds of things like mugs and sweatshirts and calendars and even trivets—but only after most of us had to have trivets explained to us.

All of that expanding happened in the late 1980s and early '90s. That was the first time we started to have brainstorm meetings about what else we could do. Companies are always having brainstorm meetings about what else they can do. That's how we got minivans and three flavors of popcorn in one tin. At one of these meetings, someone *probably* said we should do some sort of show with a character from our greeting cards.

I say "probably" because I have no real recollection of that. I get credit for the idea now because of what happened later. Did I really come up with the original idea? Not sure. And because I'm not sure, then probably not. I feel like I'd take credit for it if I could.

But, somehow, it was decided that one of our characters should be featured in a live show in Branson, Missouri.

If you've never been to Branson, it's totally worth the trip. I've seen a good deal of the Midwest, and Branson is by far one of the prettiest parts. It's right up there with Wisconsin Dells, only south and lots less snowy. It's full of people on vacation, and once those people are done boating and fishing and zip-lining, they go to shows—a wide variety of shows. There are horses that do tricks. There are Red Sea parts in a show about Moses. There are "tribute" shows featuring all kinds of music. There's a show on a boat. There are shows in an amusement park. It's a lot of shows. That's what I'm suggesting.

Another writer and I went to Branson several years ago. We saw a lot of these shows, and it seemed to us that we had a character the folks in Branson would like to see. She was a remarkably popular greeting-card character named Maxine.

By this time, Maxine had been featured on countless cards, calendars, T-shirts, mugs, puzzles, ornaments, and trivets (which we now all knew was a thing you put hot things on). She even had her own Facebook page with millions of fans.

We thought our show should be Christmas themed. We thought it should be a musical. And we thought that Maxine, a lovably grouchy old lady, would make a good Scrooge-style character.

Branson is just under four hours from Hallmark's headquarters in Kansas City if you stop for cheese. And you pretty much have to stop for cheese because if you're old enough and you're drinking coffee, you're going to stop anyway. So why not stop at a place that has more than 200 samples of cheese? You wander up and down the refrigerated display cases, and you stab interesting samples with toothpicks. Sometimes you're behind a busload of people doing the same thing. Other times it's just you and a couple of Amish families who keep to themselves. Either way, there's plenty of cheese for everybody.

In between Kansas City and cheese and Branson, we planned out how we wanted the show to go. We thought it would be funny for Maxine to work someplace where she came into contact with the public, someplace like the DMV. And she'd be mean. Then she'd meet three ghosts. Then, she'd still be mean, but slightly less so.

For me, the idea is the hard part. Once the idea is in place, the rest is just execution. So, we knew we had the main character. We'd add three ghosts, and we'd have someone for Maxine to be mean to. Eventually, she'd learn something, and there you go. Simple enough.

The other writer wrote the music. To me, that's like saying, "The other magician sawed the lady in half" while I stood there holding his top hat and gesturing toward him. He also wrote most of the lyrics. We worked together on the story itself.

I'd write some; he'd make it better. He'd write some; I'd make it better.

It was a comfortable back and forth and give and take, and we ended up with something we liked. But we also had no real idea of what we were doing.

So we enlisted a couple of Branson experts who were hugely helpful. How so? I'll give you an example. There's a song in the second act where Maxine is going from place to place with the Ghost of Christmas Present. She encounters her own family having a great time. In fact, they're singing a song about how great a time they're having. We got some friends of ours from Hallmark to record this song, along with the other songs, and we sent it to our Branson experts. (Hallmark is full of folks who can sing and play instruments. It's like a company comprised of the extended Von Trapp family.)

Anyway, the song's chorus went, "There's always room at the big ol' family table," and it makes Maxine see what she's been missing. Made perfect sense to us. When our friends sang it, it made sense to them too.

But when we sent the song to Branson, they just heard it without being able to read the lyrics. So, in as nice and friendly a way as possible (and it seems to me *everything* that happens in Branson happens that way), they asked, "Who are the Biggles?"

We said, "What?"

They said, "The Biggle family, from the song about their table. Also, why are they singing about their table?"

You see, when you hear the song, as an audience would, it does sound like a song about the Biggles. That's why we need experts. So we changed the song from "Big Ol' Family Table" to "Family Dinner Table." So far, everyone who's heard it has understood it just fine.

Those experts were also vital in helping us cast the show.

In my life up to that point, I had cast zero shows. Hard to believe, but true. Fortunately, our Branson experts knew everyone who lived in Branson. It's not a big town, and the performers all seem to either know or know *of* each other. We got to audition young and old and everything in between, all in a living room.

We had no office in Branson, and we couldn't use the theater until a week before the show began. So every audition occurred in the director's living room. No one seem surprised by this. If my neighbors were auditioning singers and actors every evening for a couple of weeks, I'd think it was strange. In Branson, it's just another night.

Of the 16 people we saw, we hired 14. Would have been 15, but there was a scheduling problem. That's how accurate our Branson experts were. They brought us people who were very good, or at least pretty good. At least that's how it seemed to me.

When you can't sing or act, everyone who can sing or act seems absolutely magical. I was in a fund-raising video once at church. I portrayed myself and was completely unconvincing. I made walking down a hallway and talking look like two things that can never happen at the same time, like swimming underwater while eating soup. Because of that, I would have cast the first 14 people to show up, no matter what. They all seemed great to me.

And I would know, because I got to see about 30 of the 35 shows during that first season. I stayed in a hotel that was a short walk from the theater and took notes during every performance. Then the directors and I would discuss the notes, and the actors would decide if they cared about them or not.

Directing, as it turns out, is a lot like coaching. You can tell your players what to do, but they're the ones on the field. Once the game starts, all you can do is watch from the sidelines and hope for the best. I had seen some theater close-up because of Christian Youth Theater, so I knew that the green room wasn't green and you're not supposed to say, "Good luck."

But Christian Youth Theater shows ran only one weekend at a time, and the oldest cast members were 18. This was a whole different ball game, to continue the sports analogy from the paragraph right before this one.

The men and women in our cast worked harder than I've ever seen anyone work. And to those of us sitting in the audience each night, they made all that hard work look easy. Our show was in the morning, and most of the cast had to leave right away, with applause ringing in their ears, for their next call time (industry lingo!)—often only 15 or 20 minutes later. Some of our cast members were in three shows a day. Three!

And the crew that worked the lights, the sound, and the house (more lingo!) had two more shows a day to do after ours was done.

I'd go back to my hotel room and write greeting cards on my laptop. Then I'd look at the room service menu and try to decide what was the least-bad thing for me to eat. There would be a meeting to discuss notes, either in person or online. My workday would end at about six. Then I'd have to figure out what to do in a town where the only people I knew were at work at their other jobs.

I watched a lot of Netflix on my tablet, and I spent a lot of time calling the front desk to ask how to get the internet in my room. "Dicey" would be the most generous description of Branson IT.

I also went to lots of shows starring the cast members of our musical, and I developed an exercise regimen: I'd walk down the hotel hallway, take the stairs to the floor below, then walk the other way and take the other stairs, all the way down and all the way up the nine floors. I got to know the hotel staff by doing this, and I got to meet a lot of nice people on vacation. My room deal included the breakfast buffet, and in six weeks I had more biscuits and more gravy than anyone needs in a lifetime. I learned to appreciate my wife even more, and I developed empathy for anyone who travels for work. Traveling seems cool only to those who don't have to do it all the time.

But the Maxine Christmas show went really well. In fact, it's still doing just fine, even without its creators there to oversee things every night.

This musical marked the start of my fourth decade at Hallmark, and I got to do something I'd never done before. That's rare on more than one count. Sometimes, not often, but sometimes, you get to see how all the things that have happened in your life up to that point come together to prepare you for something completely new and unexpected.

Those blessings we don't see coming—the ones we couldn't even imagine? Those are some of the best blessings of all.

# 63

# Banana-gelism

I was 12 or 13, sitting in an audience composed of various church youth groups, when I heard this challenge: "If every one of you can win one person to the Lord in the next year, then there will be twice as many of us here next year. And if all of *those* people win one, and it goes on and on, pretty soon, everyone on earth will be saved."

As it turned out, I was in that same gathering a year later. Our numbers had not doubled. Our group was about the same size as the year before. I knew I had not done my part, but I figured some real go-getter would have won two people, maybe three, and covered my quota. Many of us must have been thinking the same thing.

At that same meeting, I was informed that heaven would be a wonderful place except for one nagging little thing. We'd be haunted by the knowledge we had not won enough people to the Lord. Heaven's golden streets would not be crowded, and that was a bad thing. And it would be our fault. This was a great way to produce guilt, but maybe not such a great way to produce disciples.

Since then, I've been exposed to, participated in, and even led parts of several different programs—programs that are all supposed to end with everybody getting saved. I bet you know how each of these has turned out, so far.

My "youth minister years" (1.5 years, to be exact) were the worst. Our church bought notebooks and taught classes. Evangelism was set to explode. Supplied with a leader's guide, I had all the answers to the blank spaces in the instructional paragraphs. I had all the Bible verses that supported the answers.

Our mission was simple. We'd go house to house in assigned

neighborhoods and ask people, "If you died tonight, do you know where you will spend eternity?"

It's hard to believe that didn't work. The "easiest" people would answer, "I would go to heaven!"

"Terrific!" we'd say. "Thank you." Then it was on to the next house.

The next house would be less easy. The people would want to discuss the details of their faith tradition, and how they differed from other traditions. These chats were interesting (sometimes) in a seminary kind of way. But they didn't build our evangelism numbers.

The toughest households didn't want to talk about faith of any kind with anybody. They were certainly not going to discuss this topic with two strangers who showed up on their front porch. (Yes, as it was in the days of Noah, we were sent out two by two.)

I still remember one candidate asking me why God had allowed her loved one to die unexpectedly. Neither our evangelism notebook nor all of our "pregame" role-playing gave us a response to that question.

Maybe this approach worked like a charm in some places. (Perhaps "worked like a charm" sounds a little gypsy for church, but you know what I mean.) Our church's evangelism program did not explode. The people who participated in this program were the ones who always participate in such programs. They did their best. They followed the script. And life went on, pretty much like it had before.

I've also been to weekend retreats to discover a new evangelism format that promises to "change lives!" I can't even remember all the formats and plans.

I've heard about approaches that have worked in other churches—from starting evangelism-based small groups in your home to starting a soccer league so that the kids and their parents will join your church.

And then there was the banana bread gambit.

I learned that one of my coworkers was going to be moving on an upcoming weekend. This guy knew me well enough to inform me of his plans—but not well enough to ask me to help with the move. So he knew me the perfect amount.

On the Monday morning after the move, while we were in the

Hallmark break room, waiting for the coffee to finish brewing, he told me the following story.

He and his wife and kids were in midmove when neighbors dropped by with a loaf of banana bread. *How nice!* he and his wife thought. *Here we are in the midst of a challenging-at-best day, and here comes a smiling couple with delicious bread, homemade from bananas that were no longer edible in any other way.* (You have to hand it to bananas, by the way. One of our quickest-ripening fruits, they've figured out a way to extend their shelf life and maybe even become tastier in the process. Avocados could learn a thing or two from bananas.)

The smiling couple offered the banana bread and a hearty welcome to the neighborhood. Then they invited my coworker and his family to church.

"Solid move," I told myself. "Classic Banana Bread Evangelism execution. Wonder how it turned out?" (The evangelism tactic, not the bread.)

Well, what happened next is a reality that a lot of Christians live each day. Most of us are not part of a denomination noted for its homespun haircuts or clothing, or our remarkably well-crafted furniture. On Monday morning in the break room at work, we look and act much like everyone else.

That's why I found myself sitting there, horrified, while my coworker explained how disappointed and manipulated he and his wife felt by the banana bread. To them, it was nothing more than a baked bribe to get them to attend church. That evangelistic couple conveyed that they were really interested in the new neighbors only if they wanted to join them in church that Sunday.

The saddest part of the whole thing was that the other coworkers in the break room said, "Oh, yeah," before describing other breads and other methods they had been subjected to.

A common theme emerged: Christians are interested in non-Christians only as targets—as a means to bolster those evangelism numbers.

I sat there feeling like a spy. And not a very honorable spy, either, because that banana bread could have come from me.

Do Christians look at their neighborhoods as target zones? Are we driven by numbers and not relationships? I really don't think so. I can honestly say that I've never known a Christian who saw numbers first and people second—or who evaluated the success of a small group or a Sunday school class or anything else just by the total attendance.

However, we might be guilty of failing to get to know people well enough to know how they see us. That's trickier.

The kind of evangelism that truly explodes doesn't come in a notebook. It comes in the tiniest things we do and say. In the looks on our faces while we do them. Most of it happens when we're not trying so hard, when we're not looking around for "the signs." It happens when we're simply and humbly being the people God made us to be, in the places God knew we'd be someday.

The notebooks aren't bad. The retreats aren't bad. There isn't one of us who has everything figured out. Trying is always better than not trying at all.

We're supposed to be the salt of the earth. Is there salt in banana bread? I have no idea how you make it. But I know the salt in other things is usually just a little bit, doing a little bit. And making a big difference.

# 64

# Date Night!

When you're young, you have romantic notions. One of these notions is that you'll never have to do something so mechanical and inorganic as scheduling a "date night" with your beloved person.

That's a romantic notion about romantic notions, and like most of them, it doesn't hold up in the harsh light of the combined forces of schedules and laziness.

Museum exhibits, gallery openings, concerts, plays, poetry readings, and Civil War reenactments—these are just some of the things that young me saw not-so-young me doing as a married person.

Staring into each other's eyes and sharing our deepest feelings was right up there too. My wife and I would return from a Russian Impressionist art show opening (if that's a thing) and reflect on how it moved us. Whenever we were together, the sparks would be visible from space. Other couples would look at us with a mixture of awe and envy that we'd try, and fail, not to notice. We would pity them, and that sorrow would be the only sigh in our otherwise buoyant, cloud-floating-life of love.

Or not so much. And it's mostly my fault. When we have an open night, it's difficult to get me to leave the house. (I especially don't want to go out on "school nights," even though our kids have long since matriculated and no longer live at home.)

Going to see a friend's kid, whom I barely know, in an experimental dance recital (not making this up) is not the winch that is going to pull me off my sofa. We live in the suburbs, and my work is downtown—where the cool things are happening. It's also where I *don't* want to go, especially on the weekend. That's because driving toward work but not getting paid makes no sense to me. None at all. It's like being 12 and riding your bike past the school in the summer.

There are two things I will gladly do. (Everything else requires a stern pep talk—either from myself or from someone I married.)

I'll always go see my son play live music. There isn't anything else like that. I can tell already that I'll also gladly go see my grandkids in anything they do, but they won't be as good as my son is at music, at least not for a long time.

The other thing is movies. Really doesn't matter much which movie. If you made a movie and it's playing in a big theater, I'll go see it.

However, if you made an indie art-house documentary? Well, you weren't thinking of me when you made it, were you? Kind of selfish of you.

Otherwise, I'll go. I'll go see an action movie, a romantic comedy, a regular comedy, a drama, and in special circumstances, like a national holiday, musicals.

So that sounds like a date, right? Here's the thing though: When you know you like movies for movies' sake—and you can get an early afternoon ticket for half price—then why go at night?

And here's the thing about theaters: They are dark and have no windows. If the movie can't get you over the fact that it's four thirty and sunny outside, it's not much of a movie. And once the movie ends, there's probably a half-price appetizer deal somewhere nearby.

If you grew up in the Depression, you're nodding your gray head right now. I did not grow up in the Depression, but it kind of kills me to pay full price for a movie or a burrito. Again, on national holidays I'm game. If people are going and doing a thing, I'll go and I'll do.

However, I didn't care about gallery openings when I was 27, so I don't know what made me think I would in the decades to follow.

"There's a two-appetizers-and-one-entrée-for-20-bucks deal that's happening in 750 restaurants across America! It is an awesome deal. Try the jalapeño poppers!" I get that this is not how the sexy people talk. It's how they talk at places where you have to be 55 or better to live there, and that's okay with me.

Is it a cliché to say that date night is more about what's in our hearts than what's on our plates? Of course it is. It's also true. There are times when Lana and I put on a recorded episode of a show where people are passionately choosing backsplash tile. Then we just sit there and disagree with their insistence on the herringbone pattern. We know we are exactly where we want to be and we're doing exactly what we want to do—because of whom we're doing it with.

The 27-year-old me would not approve, but he's nowhere near as smart as current me. (And he'd be too busy enjoying the jalapeño poppers to complain. They really are amazing.)

# 65

# Write Now

One of my summer jobs involved hanging drywall as well as taping it. Hanging drywall boards means you cut them to size and nail them to the frame of the house. Thicker, longer boards are used for fire code reasons in some parts of the house (such as the garage ceiling). That's how I found myself standing on a scaffold that was 14 feet above a concrete floor and holding one end of a 100-pound sheet of drywall. Also, it was 100 degrees outside. Garages, as you may know, do not come with air conditioning. Heat, as you may know, rises in places like tall garages. Hanging that ceiling was a hard job. Writing is not a hard job, not compared to that.

I have a friend who's an air traffic controller. As the title suggests, he controls the traffic…in the air. If he makes a mistake, planes crash into each other. That's a hard job. Writing is not a hard job, not compared to that.

For the most part, writing is a pretty fun job. Yes, carpal tunnel syndrome is a constant threat, and all of your saved data could go wherever all the saved data goes when you realize you really were not saving it at all. That can happen.

Also, people can look at your writing and not think much of it. I can promise you that happens. When it does, you think about taping drywall and how you were 35 years younger when you did that, and it wasn't easy. Then you tell yourself, "I'm going to write something *else* and hope people like that."

I hope you've like this book. And I hope that maybe for a little bit you laughed—or at least chuckled. Maybe you remembered something from your past that was kind of like mine. Or maybe it was very different from mine, but still, you remembered something warmly for a bit.

When you look back, and when you look around, I hope you see God's hand in your life, in the lives of those around you, and in the world you know and influence. And I hope you try to laugh more, or at least chuckle. Maybe you'll go do some little things to make your world a little better.

Writing is not a hard job, not compared to that.

# About the Author

**Dan Taylor** is a preacher's kid and a former youth pastor who's been writing humor books and other products for Hallmark for more than 30 years. He helped launch Hallmark's Shoebox brand of greeting cards, as well as the popular character "Maxine." As a husband, parent, church leader, and, of course, greeting card writer, Dan has seen the funny side of just about everything.

This is a book about things that have happened to Dan—good, less good, and sometimes hilariously not good at all. It's about him, but you'll see yourself in it as well. Sometimes you'll think, *Oh, I would have handled that much better than Dan did.* Other times you'll think, *Hmm... what he did there is interesting, but also wrong.* And every now and then you'll think, *That was really funny! That should be in a book!*

We thought so too, and this is that book. See how things work together for the funny?

To learn more about Harvest House books and
to read sample chapters, visit our website:

**www.harvesthousepublishers.com**

**HARVEST HOUSE PUBLISHERS**
EUGENE, OREGON